Contents

D1556426

Editorial

Technology and money are seen by many as the two 'engines of progress' of world development (Crewe and Harrison 1998, 30). The delivery of new technologies designed in the North to the South has been viewed by governments and non-government organisations (NGOs) of all political persuasions as the key to economic and social development. However, women's experiences of technological innovation have shown that this is a gross over-simplification. While technologies of different kinds, in varying social contexts, offer opportunities to challenge existing barriers to economic, social, and political participation, they can also consolidate or worsen existing power imbalances. This collection of articles considers gender relations in the light of the use and adaptation of indigenous technologies, and the 'technical transfer' of Northern-designed technologies into Southern contexts. Writers here focus on a wide array of technologies, including those intended to enable women to generate income and increase agricultural production; to save their labour in home-based tasks; to enable them to control their fertility; and to communicate using computer technology.

The definition of 'technology' used in this collection is a broad one. Technology can be defined as an object which does something that works or helps (Everts 1998, 5). Gender and development research and activism have emphasised the importance of the technical skills and knowledge required to use the technology, and the social situation in which this use occurs. These are the key factors which determine the economic and social impact of a technology on the women and men who design, build, purchase, and use it. Writers here give attention to all these elements.

'Progress', modernity, and technology

For the past 300 years, societies have been judged as progressive or backward depending on their knowledge of European science and technology (Crewe and Harrison 1998). As Maggie Foster describes in her article, critiques of the transfer of mainstream 'modern' technology began to gain ground in the 1960s and 1970s. A focus on mostly large-scale, technically sophisticated technologies in urban industrial settings gave way to concerns to meet the needs of rural dwellers for 'appropriate' technology. Appropriateness was judged according to criteria such as small scale, low complexity, and easy maintenance. While this shift sounds — and is still rated as — a milestone in development thought and practice, the judges who deemed technologies 'appropriate' or otherwise were still not the women and men who would use or adapt them, but Northern, predominantly male, experts. Their knowledge continued to be seen as superior to that of the producers and users of indigenous technologies: 'we develop technologies which are very much better than the decayed, mediaeval technologies of the poor' (Schumacher 1975, quoted in Crewe and Harrison 1998, 33).

A quarter of a century later, some commentators are drawing parallels between these ideas of modern technologies as the key to development, and those currently being made about information and communications technologies (ICT), including the Internet. Promises of new opportunities for wealth and equality through ICT are matched by dire warnings of the dangers of non-participation in the ICT revolution. For these commentators, 'the ICT hype merely replaces the classical opiate of religion and the modernist idea of progress' (Inayatullah and Milojevic 1999, 78, discussing the work of Kevin Robbins).

Acknowledging women's skills in technology

While the precise impact of the transfer of technology from Northern to Southern contexts is context-specific, there is considerable evidence that it has disadvantaged women (Everts 1998). The association of progress and power with Northern-designed technology was reproduced in Southern communities, where men were quick to see the advantages of controlling new technology. The change from using indigenous technologies to those designed in the North meant a challenge to the gender division of labour, and in some cases to women losing control of both technological processes and the end product. A growing outcry against the marginalisation of women from the benefits of development during the United Nations Decade for Women (1976-85) stimulated interest in women's role vis-à-vis technology — not only as users, but as innovators and producers.

Male technologists working for development organisations have often abetted this growing male control over technology, through seeking out male members of the communities where they work. Misconceptions about women's roles in communities throughout the world, based on Northern ideals of domesticity, have encouraged a view of women as dependent on men's labour. Since the 1970s, feminist researchers have offered abundant evidence to Northern development organisations to contradict this stereotype. In fact, women are skilled family providers, who perform whatever work is necessary, paid or unpaid, to meet their dependents' needs. Such research — a key part of which focused on the technology women used — recorded and raised awareness of women's multiple roles in production and reproduction (Carr 1984). Gender analysis of women's uses of technologies shows that 'reproductive' and 'productive' tasks are often impossible to distinguish, since making a living may involve performing the same tasks with the same technologies — for example, food-processing — for both subsistence and income-generating purposes.

The valuable technological skills and knowledge which women do possess have often gone unrecognised and unvalued (Appleton 1995, 8). 'It is important to consider not only the content of what people know, but the knowledge systems within which information is used, because such systems underlie processes of problem diagnosis, experimentation and innovation' (ibid., 9). In her article, Rachel Humphreys discusses the various ways in which the skills that women in northern Thailand traditionally employ in weaving are undervalued. Industrialists exploit these skills in factory assembly lines, while NGOs promote women's 'traditional' craft work as an alternative to urban migration, at the same time perpetuating gender stereotypes of 'good women' who stay at home and weave. Humphreys argues that in a context

4

of precarious markets and a widespread need for income, a forward-looking strategy would be to raise public awareness and offer women weavers opportunities to formalise, and upgrade, their skills.

Many discussions of technology from a gender perspective focus on women's 'economic empowerment' (Everts 1998, 4). If women's time is generally taken up in work which does not bring in income, they may prefer to reduce their existing workload in order to take on work which brings in money. While the relationship between income generation and intra-household power relations is a very complex one, projects and programmes for women which are informed by a commitment to changing gender power relations tend to focus on the fact that money gives women the choice whether to go or to stay.

Integrating gender concerns into technical interventions

A major barrier to acknowledging women's link with technology has been the widespread assumption that an understanding of mechanical engineering and associated technical and scientific subjects cannot exist in the absence of Northern-style formal education, which has always been more accessible to men. As Radhika Gajjala and Annapurna Mamidipudi show in their article on textile and information and communications (ICT) technologies, biases about the 'backwardness' of women and of developing countries have dealt Southern women a double blow. Such prejudice has deeply influenced the organisations which promote technology in development.

While development agencies whose work focuses on technology transfer may assert that they have targeted women as users of technology extensively over the past two decades, the underlying aim of such work has not always been to promote gender equity. A key part of it has instead expected on women to deliver results to suit other

agendas. For example, in the 1970s environmental concerns about deforestation led to projects which aimed to make women use fuel-efficient stoves in their role as carers for families. Some of this work was unsuccessful, but much of it has had a very positive impact on women by reducing the time spent on cooking. However, these programmes have lost the support of donors, since their effect on reducing fuel consumption has been much less clear (Crewe and Harrison 1998). Another much-documented recognition of women users of technology has occurred in population control. Gill Gordon and Katie Chapman's article discusses the different feminist views of the impact on women and gender relations of 'reproductive technologies' which control conception and, importantly in this era of HIV/AIDS, the spread of sexually-transmitted diseases (STDs). Their article discusses a programme which promoted knowledge about and use of contraceptive technologies in rural Zambia, in the context of changing gender power relations.

Another rationale for targeting women in development interventions has been to depict them as 'the poorest of the poor'. Commitment to poverty alleviation has enabled many development programmes to work with women without overtly challenging unequal power relations, which are intrinsically linked to women's experience of day-to-day poverty. This focus recognises women as producers in agriculture and small-scale commodity production, and acknowledges their dual role here and inside the household. Typically focusing on making productive work more productive, and reproductive work easier, this approach aims to improve women's lives without overtly challenging 'culture' and the gender division of labour. In their article, Joyce Otsyina and Diana Rosenberg focus on the work of a Tanzanian technology programme sponsored by government and international donors, which took this approach.

During the 1990s, a major focus for gender and development policy and practice has been power relations between women and men, in the family and in the public sphere. There have been widespread calls for organisational change, to ensure that our organisations are shaped by a commitment to gender equity and the rights of women (Goetz 1998). Only once this has been achieved, can organisations start to develop projects which challenge women's marginalisation on grounds of intrinsic justice, rather than simple pragmatism. In her article, Maggie Foster argues that it is particularly difficult to convince organisations which focus on technology to see women's rights as their concern, because of the Northern tradition of seeing technical and social fields of study as distinct from each other, and the association of technical subjects with men. Maya Prabhu's article analyses the ways in which her organisation has addressed the need to change its own identity in order to ensure that women as well as men are reached in the communities where organisations work.

Gender, technology, and communications

During the past decade, there has been a renewed interest in the power of communications and information exchange as an engine for development, coinciding with the growth of personal computing and telecommunications, and the 'virtual world' created as a result. Radhika Gajjala and Annapurna Mamidipudi exchange their views on the Internet, while Heather Schreiner looks at telecentres, which offer more familiar ways of electronic communications including radio and telephone in addition in Internet access. Currently, discussion of the scope of the Internet to bring about understanding between Southern and Northern women and men, to exchange information, and to offer marketing and lobbying opportunities,

are matched only by dire predictions of the marginalisation and oppression awaiting those who are not linked up. What is the real scope of these new technologies in offering empowerment for women living in poverty in South and North?

Radhika Gajjala and Annapurna Mamidipudi's article (written as an Internet dialogue between two authors based in North America and India) challenges simplistic ideas about what constitutes 'modern' technology, drawing a parallel between debates on ICT and the textile industry. In both, they argue, Southern women are seen as backward and their traditional skills and knowledge derided. In fact, Southern women innovate and adapt technologies as they have always done, integrating those from other cultures into their own. This dynamic approach to technology proves that distinctions between what is 'traditional' and what is 'modern' are meaningless and patronising. While the Internet definitely offers opportunities for discussion and debate, which may lead to a better understanding between people living in different contexts of wealth and poverty across the world, such prejudices will not be challenged unless Southern women actually shape their Internet 'spaces', and Northerners listen and question their own assumptions about the South. In short, 'with all the rhetoric about the need to liberate "unheard voices", we miss an essential point: those voices have been talking all along. The question is who is listening' (Agustin 1999, 155).

Heather Schreiner's article, a case study of a pioneering telecentre project in rural South Africa, provides a 'reality check' of a different kind regarding women's use of new communications technologies. The realities of setting up and maintaining sophisticated and expensive machinery in a developing country means that such centres are seen by many as an impossible dream. In one conference in Ethiopia in 1998, South African participants who discussed their country's experience were told that they did not understand the realities of their neighbours (ECA Conference, Addis Ababa, May 1998). At a recent estimate, trade relations between unequal economies mean that an information economy can trade one copy of word-processing software for 2,000 kilos of African coffee (Tandon 1999, 134).

A common concern for several writers in this issue, including Heather Schreiner and Maya Prabhu, is the scope for development practitioners to work in partnership with the private sector in order to make it possible to afford technical innovation, and render it sustainable. This is a particularly challenging idea for many NGOs whose left-wing political roots encourage them to reject the idea of working for profit with individuals. However, these debates are increasingly common, and opinions are much less polarised than hitherto: 'the idea is that if we were to hop on to the train of the market, and maybe slightly redirect some of the actors, and if necessary jump off in time, we would arrive much faster at where we want to be' (Everts 1998, 69).

Using 'hard' and 'soft' communications technologies

Some contributions here consider the ways in which the older technologies of electronic and print communications have been used, both positively and negatively, from a gender perspective. In Heather Schreiner's article, all the electronic methods of communicating offered in the telecentre were new to the surrounding community; computers are offered alongside telephones and photocopiers, but the telephone proved most popular. Heather Schreiner points out that women do not as yet perceive a need to use them: while they are well aware of the advantages of using telecommunications to overcome geographical distances, their migrant male partners are at the other end of the telephone, not the computer. Unless

there is a practical rationale for using new technology, busy women who view computer technology as alien and off-putting are unlikely to see the point of exploring it — although, as Schreiner reports, many recognise it as a valuable future resource. Echoing the case study from South Africa, Southern women who participated in a research survey by the Association for Progressive Communications (APC) listed the following obstacles to using computer technoloy: limited access to the Internet, time consumption, information overload, language constraints, lack of privacy or security, skill deficiencies, and alienation (Farwell et al., 1998).

Another communications technology discussed in this collection is radio. For many years, radio was in vogue as a valuable method of popular education and distance learning, promoting skills and knowledge for development over great distances in a relatively accessible form. However, many studies in North and South have also documented the role of the mass media in reflecting existing sexist stereotypes about women and men. Charles Chilimampunga provides an entertaining yet incisive case study of radio advertising in Malawi, as a reminder that this issue remains highly topical. Gill Gordon and Katie Chapman's article reflects current interest in communications technologies as a key to promoting social development goals and participatory methods of development. In their case study of reproductive health technologies in Zambia, they discuss the use of the 'soft' technologies of interactive learning to promote these, as an alternative to the 'hard' technologies of radio, video, and print. Continuing this theme, Joyce Otsyina and Diana Rosenberg's article looks at different methods of communication used in a rural community in Tanzania to promote the use of improved stoves and agricultural techniques.

Conclusion

In assessing the impact on poverty of technology-focused development projects, gender analysis confirms the critical importance to women of having access to technology, as well as control over the conditions of production, and confident knowledge of the process. Despite the efforts of gender and development researchers, practitioners, and policy-makers over the past 30 years to chart and promote women's skills as users of technology, 'in the invention and development of technology, women's technical expertise has been displaced with particular efficacy' (Crewe and Harrison 1998, 34). As we enter the twenty-first century, we have another chance to reject the deep-rooted prejudices which associate women, and the South, with backwardness and tradition, and men and the North with progress and modernity. These stereotypes, rooted in precolonial assumptions about the superiority of European 'civilisation', are currently being recast in the context of debates on the possibilities offered for 'progress' and 'learning' by electronic methods of communications, including computers.

In her article, Maggie Foster points out that a first step for organisations which wish to ensure that in future women gain access to truly appropriate technologies is to reject such stereotypes, and recognise women's role as existing and potential innovators of technology. Development workers have long pointed out that to discover what is truly appropriate, it is necessary to consult the users. However, in order to do this, 'some sort of "culture-change" among development workers may be required' (Everts 1998, 38). A number of suggestions are put forward by contributors here, ranging from organisational change in NGOs to working with partners in the private sector. It is possible that market mechanisms may enable development workers to promote sustainable technical change more widely. However, as Maya Prabhu's article discusses, this approach raises further essential questions regarding women as consumers, which 'leads to the need for insight into intra-household dynamics in order to discover the niches of women's autonomy' (Everts 1998, 83).

References

Agustin, L (1999) 'They speak, but who listens?' in Harcourt, W (ed.).

Appleton, H (1995) *Do it Herself: Women and technical innovation*, IT Publications, London.

Carr, M (1984) *Blacksmith, Baker, Roofing-sheet Maker: Employment for rural women in developing countries*, IT Publications, London.

Crewe, E and Harrison, E (1998) *Whose Development? An ethnography of aid*, Zed Books, London.

Everts, S (1998) *Gender and Technology: Empowering women, engendering development*, Zed Books, London.

Farwell, E, Wood, P, James, M, and Banks, K (1999) 'Global Networking for Change: experiences from the APC Women's Programme', in Harcourt, W (ed.).

Goetz, A-M (1998) *Getting institutions right for women in development*, Zed Books, London.

Harcourt, W (ed.) (1999) *Women@Internet: Creating New Cultures in Cyberspace*, Zed Books, London.

Inayatullah, S and Milojevic, I (1999) 'Exclusion and Communication in the Information Era: From silences to global conversations', in Harcourt, W (ed.).

Schumacher, E (1973) *Small is Beautiful: a study of economics as if people mattered*, Abacus, London.

Tandon, N (1999) 'Global Business, National Politics, Community Planning: Are women building the linkages?', in Harcourt, W (ed.).

Cyberfeminism, technology, and international 'development'

Radhika Gajjala and Annapurna Mamidipudi[1]

Feminists from diverse backgrounds are considering the implications of the spread of Internet technology, and questioning its benefits for women in developing countries. Apart from having access to the Internet, women must also be able to define the content and shape of cyberspace.

The simplest way to describe the term 'cyberfeminism' might be that it refers to women using Internet technology for something other than shopping via the Internet or browsing the world-wide web[2]. One could also say that cyberfeminism is feminism in relation to 'cyberspace'. Cyberspace is 'informational data space made available by electrical circuits and computer networks' (Vitanza 1999, 5). In other words, cyberspace refers to the 'spaces', or opportunities, for social interaction provided by computers, modems, satellites, and telephone lines — what we have come to call 'the Internet'. Even though there are several approaches to cyberfeminism, cyberfeminists share the belief that women should take control of and appropriate the use of Internet technologies in an attempt to empower themselves. The idea that the Internet can be empowering to individuals and communities who are under-privileged is based on the notion of scientific and technological progress alleviating human suffering, offering the chance of a better material and emotional quality of life. In this article, we make conceptual links between 'old' and 'new' technologies within contexts of globalisation[3], third-world development, and the empowerment of women. We wish to question the idea of 'progress' and 'development' as the inevitable result of science and technology, and develop a critique of the top-down approach to technology transfer from the Northern to the Southern hemisphere. There are two questions of central importance: First, will women in the South be able (allowed) to use new technologies under conditions that are contextually empowering to them, because they are defined by women themselves? Second, within which Internet-based contexts can women from the South truly be heard? How can they define the conditions under which they can interact on-line[4], to enable them to form coalitions and collaborate, aiming to transform social, cultural, and political structures?

The Internet and 'development'

Cyberfeminists urge women all over the world to learn how to use computers, to get 'connected'[5], and to use the Internet as a tool for feminist causes and individual empowerment. However, ensuring that women are empowered by new technology requires us to investigate issues which are far more complex than merely providing material access to the latest technologies. The Internet has fascinated many activists and scholars because of its potential to connect people all across the world in a way that has never been possible before. Individuals can publish written material instantaneously, and broadcast information to remote locations. Observers predict that it will cause unprecedented and radical change in the way human beings conduct business and social activities. In much of the North, as well as in some materially privileged sections of societies in the South, the Internet is celebrated as a tool for enhancing world-wide democracy. The Internet and its associated technologies are touted as great equalisers, which will help bridge gaps between social groups: the 'haves' and the 'have-nots', and men and women.

Since the Second World War, development — in the sense of transferring and 'diffusing' northern forms of scientific and technological 'progress', knowledge, and modes of production and consumption, from the industrialised north into southern contexts — has been seen by many as the one over-arching solution to poverty and inequality around the world. Much of the current literature, as well as media representations of the so-called under-developed world, reinforces this discourse of 'development' and 'under-development'. As scholars such as Edward Said (1978) have pointed out, this process is also apparent in the context of colonialism, when the production of knowledge about the colonised nations served the colonisers in justifying their project.

What, then, does it mean to say that the Internet and technology are feminist issues for women in developing nations, when the project of development in itself is saddled with colonial baggage? In order to examine whether women in these contexts are indeed going to realise empowerment through the use of technology, we need to understand the complexity of the obstacles they face, by considering the ways in which the conditions of their lives are determined by unequal power relations at local and global levels.

The form of this article

In the following, we each describe our engagement with cyberfeminisms, development, and new technology, and discuss some of the problems that we encounter in our efforts. Both of us have interacted quite extensively using the Internet, where our interactions occasionally overlap when we engage in discussions and creative exchanges with others[6]. One of us, Annapurna Mamidipudi, is also involved with an NGO working with traditional handloom weavers in south India. The other, Radhika Gajjala, works within academia, and creates and runs on-line 'discussion lists'[7] and websites from her North American geographical location, aiming to create spaces that enable dialogue and collaboration among women with access to the internet all over the world. This paper was written via the Internet, across a fairly vast geographical distance of approximately 10,000 miles. We have written the article as a dialogue, to make our individual voices and locations apparent. This unconventional form and method seems appropriate for our subject matter: a belief in the possibilities of dialogue and collaboration across geographical boundaries offered by this medium of the future. We do not consider either of us to represent the North or the South, 'theory' or 'practice'; each of us will use her professional and personal experience of technology within both 'first world' and 'third-world' contexts. We share caste, class, national, and religious affiliations, but once again, neither of us are representative Indian women.

Annapurna Mamidipudi:

As a field-worker in an organisation which focuses on the development and use of environment-friendly dyes for textile production, I am part of a team that has been successfully introducing and transferring the technology of non-chemical natural dyes to clients. The course we offer is comprehensive; it includes training in botany and dye-material cultivation patterns, concepts of eco-friendly technology, actual dyeing techniques and tools, specific methodology for further research, aesthetics, and market research. While the service we provide is similar to that of any professional consultancy, a crucial difference is that we cater solely to traditional handloom weavers; our trainees, sponsors and manufacturers are all artisans, men and women from traditional weaving communities.

The craft of traditional natural dyeing is based on sophisticated knowledge that has been passed down from generation to generation of artisans. The end-product created by these artisans is exquisite hand-loomed cloth, woven of yarn hand-spun from local cotton by women in remote Indian villages, dyed in the vibrant colours of indigo and madder. This has been exported all over the world from pre-colonial times onwards. One might well ask, why should a skill that has been passed down successfully over so many generations suddenly need technical consultants like me for training?

Radhika Gajjala:

I am a producer, first, of theory concerned with culture, post-colonialism, and feminism. I am in continuous dialogue with women from non-privileged and non-western locations, examining the experience of activists like Annapurna, and collaborating with men and women from the South. I rely to a large extent on having access to knowledge through Northern technology and power structures, but I am not blind to the fact that these power structures oppress women and men living in poverty in both North and South.

My second role as a producer is in creating electronic 'spaces' which are used by people of different identities to express themselves and talk to each other[8]. The Spoon Collective[9], started in 1994, is 'dedicated to promoting discussion of philosophical and political issues' (http://lists.village.virginia.edu/~spoons). The Spoon Collective was started in 1994, and I entered it in 1995, volunteering to co-moderate two 'discussion lists'. I set up two further discussion lists in 1995 and 1996, which I will mention later in this article.

While members of the Spoon Collective have different individual aims in belonging to the Collective, I believe that all of us are interested in the possibilities of activism through electronic communications. All of us have set up, and continue to moderate, discussion lists that implicitly question the global status quo, in one way or another. One member of the collective said, 'One way in which we conceptualise what we do is by talking about thinking [and writing/speaking on-line] as a civic, public activity'. As is characteristic of much Internet-based activity (whether activist, personal, or commercial), our goals and our actual output are constantly evaluated. We ceaselessly discuss their impact on society and culture. For example, what determines whether a list 'works' or not? The volume of messages exchanged? The quality of information or discussion? But how would 'quality' be defined? Do we determine the success of the list by the number of members who subscribe to it? Or by the number of members who participate by sending messages? By the number of websites that have links to our list-archives or the Spoon Collective website? How can we tell from this how many people we really reach?

In order to start up discussion lists, and construct websites, I had to teach myself sufficient programming and computer-related skills to be able to manage the technical side. My background as creative writer and student in the humanities had not trained me for the technical aspects of being an active producer on-line, and my knowledge is mostly self-taught. Later in this article, I will discuss my e-mail lists as part of an effort to try and facilitate collaborations between feminists across vast geographical boundaries. What scope is there for them to discuss and assert their differences on an equal basis, within these electronic social spaces which are themselves based in unequal economic, social and cultural relations? In a sense I suppose my on-line ventures could be called 'cyberfeminist' investigations.

Annapurna:

Until the nineteenth century, most of the weaving industry in the area where I work was shaped by the demands of local consumers. Chinnur is a little village in Adilabad, in an interior region of the Deccan plateau in South India. There used to be a large concentration of weavers with a reputation for excellence in this area. Their reputation was based on three things: the skill of the farmers in producing different varieties of cotton; the ability of different groups of people to work together and process the cotton; and, finally, the wealth of knowledge of dyes and techniques that added aesthetic value to utility. Different castes and communities were inter-linked in occupational, as well as social relationships, exchanging services and materials, creating a strong local market economy which was entrenched in the traditions and rituals of daily life. For example, during specific seasons or events, women of leisure from non-weaving communities spun, exchanging spun yarn for sarees (Uzramma 1995).

However, the development of chemical dyes almost 100 years ago in Europe had a calamitous effect on traditional Indian dyeing practices. Processes which were the pride of the textile industry of this country were abandoned and replaced by chemical dyes. Even in remote Chinnur, the spreading wave of modern science changed people's perceptions of traditional technology; they now saw it as outmoded, and this resulted in almost total erasure of knowledge of the traditional processes within these communities.

Europeans had started to document the local dyeing and weaving activities in the eighteenth century; Indians themselves continued this up to the early twentieth century, in a bid to preserve knowledge. But this process meant that knowledge which had been firmly in the domain of practice of the artisans was now converted into textual information, and shifted the ownership of the knowledge to those able to 'study', rather than those who 'do'.

As the outside world mutated into a global village, the organic processes of the traditional artisan weaver turned full cycle, back to popularity when the colour of neeli (indigo) caught the imagination of ecology-conscious consumers in the late 1970s. But even while the self-congratulatory back-patting went on among the nationalists and intellectuals, the weavers had internalised information about 'modern' chemical technology. Just as they had begun to find a footing in the market, their practical knowledge was again found wanting. The only available information about vegetable dyes was documented in the language of the colonisers, codified, and placed in libraries or museums, inaccessible to the traditional practitioners from whom the information had been gathered in the first instance. Thus, although it looked as if a demand had been created for their product, in reality this further reinforced the image of weavers' technology as needful of input from outside experts, in the weavers' own minds as well as in those of others.

Today, in most descriptions of the hand-loom industry, the traditional weaver is seen as an object of charity, who can survive only through government handouts or patronage from social elites. Yet their 'sunset' industry — as it was referred to by a top official in the Department of Handloom and Textiles in charge of formulating strategy for this industry (personal communication, 1999) — has the second largest number of practitioners in India, farming employing the greatest number. For the men and women engaged in weaving in villages across India, the journey from traditional neeli (indigo) to modern naphthol (chemical) dyes has meant a journey from self-sufficiency to dependence, self-respect to subordination; in short, a journey to 'primitivity'.

Radhika:

Most highly-educated women from the third world, whether or not we live in the North, experience a parallel journey to 'primitivity' in the sense Annapurna uses above. In part, this happens through acquiring western-style education and professional status, which is not often an autonomous personal choice. No woman of the third world has the luxury of not choosing to be westernised if she aspires to be heard, or even simply to achieve a level of material freedom, comfort, and luxury within global structures of power. Many of us have 'made it' within westernised professional systems, and have enjoyed the status of the representative third-world woman within global structures of power. Yet, as a result of our education and professional status, we are not representative, although we are of the third world, and our stories are not those of many truly under-privileged women in third-world locations.

Often, we meet other people's expectations by taking on the role of victims of third-world cultures, or, alternatively, victors who have 'survived' our backgrounds. Yet, when we refuse these roles allotted to us, some feminists from Northern backgrounds suggest our

experiences don't 'count', since we are not 'real' third-world women. Even as we demonstrate our potential by attaining the level of education and 'westernisation' required to become powerful within global structures, we are silenced once again.

Annapurna:

Outside the house of one of the weavers in the village of Chinnur is a chalk-written address board in English. It says: 'Venkatesh U.S., Weavers' Colony, Chinnur'. The initials U.S. after this man's name stand for 'Unskilled Labour': a powerful statement on how an expert weaver chooses to categorise himself. This classification in the government records, he hopes, will make him eligible for a low-grade job in a government office.

I first came here as one of a team of field workers from an NGO which offered marketing support to craft groups. Natural dyeing seemed an option which would add value to the cotton cloth, and which would also eventually decrease weavers' dependence on a fickle market and centralised raw material supply systems. We ourselves did not know the technology, but we were optimistic about the chance of reviving it, provided there was active participation on the part of producer groups.

Transferring the technology of natural dyeing to the field presented many challenges. The sources of information available were texts — some of them 300 years old — noting original processes of artisan practice. Some scholars had researched fragments of the old processes, and some practitioners recalled parts of them. We needed historians to access information from libraries where the documentation was kept; we then needed dyeing experts to interpret the recipes, botanists to participate in the process of identifying materials, engineers to create appropriate technology to ensure fastness and brightness in colours, and chemical technologists to interpret the techniques and demystify processes that had been inter-linked with ways of life that were sometimes centuries old. Making scientists of the weavers, we had to help them re-interpret information to suit their changed environment and resources. We did not want to impose on them— in the name of traditional technology — processes that would place demands on them which would be more oppressive than toxic chemical dyes. The innate capability and skill of the weavers made this seemingly impossible task feasible, and success came five years later, when we produced a range of colours and dyeing techniques that withstood the most stringent of quality tests. A group of dyer-weavers now acted as resource people in workshops held by us to train other groups.

Our clients today are confident weavers who come back to us time and again, to participate in the effort to empower more and more artisan groups by sharing information on a technology that has emerged from their efforts on the field.

In Chinnur lives Venkatavva, whose husband is one of a group of six weavers who decided that they would take the risk of inviting an outside agency to help them become self-sufficient. When we first visited Chinnur eight years ago, Venkatavva was unable to offer us any hospitality. Her three-year-old daughter's staple drink was weak coffee, drunk without milk. There was no food to be offered to visitors who turned up once the morning meal was past. Today, she entertains buyers from Europe, while listening to her husband tell the story of his successes. Her eyes are bright with laughter when she remembers less successful experiments which resulted in pale and fugitive colours, and irate customers. She points proudly to the shirt that her husband Odellu wears today, which he himself has woven. The journey from chemical technology to the indigo vat, from dearth to bounty, from apathy to laughter

— this is her journey. In this context, which technology is traditional and which modern? Who is to decide which one is the road to empowerment and self-respect?

Radhika:

My journey to 'modernity' began with an increasing awareness of my own ignorance, and of the contradictions and injustices which exist within the Northern educational system. I refuse to be either a 'victim' or a 'victor', and continue to hope that through dialogue, women, men and children from different backgrounds throughout the world can work together to overcome injustice.

In late 1995, when I started my first Internet discussion list, access to the Internet was limited mainly to men and women from the North. (This is the case even now, although there are more men and women from the South who use the Internet). I started the third-world women discussion list partly as a result of my frustration with what I saw as a lack of political commitment and exchange within some women-centred lists. I was frustrated with the way in which topics were discussed. Even in those instances where women and men from the South had access, they came from a particular class background. I was also frustrated with the way people represented themselves. In my opinion, some were too eager to be 'ideal native informants' for Northern audiences. Southern participants used the Internet as an opportunity to perform to a Northern audience and receive favours for sufficiently western, or appropriately exotic, performances. Even discussion lists and web-sites that claimed to be critical and feminist sometimes fell into this trap (possibly, my own lists and websites do so, too).

It was important to me at the time I started the third-world-women list, and continues to be now, that a conscious effort should be made to be critical and self-reflexive. My second list, Sa-cyborgs, was started with a similar goal in mind, but the focus of this list is an interactive exchange of creative writing in relation to gender, race, class and geographical location. Both lists were formed in the recognition that acts of representation are political.

One of the main purposes of both my Internet discussion lists is to facilitate connections between third-world activists and scholars located within, and outside, US academic institutions. I hope that this dialogue will result in collaborative work by and for women living in under-privileged and oppressive conditions, in North and South. My lists are humble efforts which form a small section of the larger efforts being made by women all over the world. Whether they have been successful in any sense is not for me to say. There are many feminists and activists using the Internet in far more effective ways, and examples of these can be seen all over the world-wide web (see http://www.igc.apc.org/vsister/res/index.html for some examples).

Annapurna:

Women who tussle with the question of how to define their class and Northern or Southern identity on the Internet are a privileged few. Questions relevant to women to whom Internet technology is being touted as the route to empowerment, might ask: 'but who has the Internet empowered? How has this happened? How relevant is this process for women like Venkatavva?'.

Venkatavva has seen the advent of roads, cars, telephones, and television in the short 30 years of her life, and understands the advantages, the disadvantages, and the illusion of access that these give her. In a land of faulty cables and unpredictable electricity supply, her children only drink milk on the days that the bus doesn't run, because on those days the milk in the village can't be taken to the city to be sold, and isn't worth any money.

Modern technology holds no bogies for her; she has choices that many women in the north don't have access to. On days the electricity fails she watches the traditional story-telling enacted in the village square instead of the distant Santa Barbara on television. The quality and quantity of the choices available to her are based as much on the failure of technology, as on its success. So would modern technology be working towards more quality and quantity in choice, or less?

As an activist working in developing technology for her I can only say this: let her have access to the Internet — why should this be barred when other aspects of modern life are imposed, from Western consumer goods, to twentieth-century diseases such as HIV/AIDS. But let it not be assumed that the Internet will empower her. Otherwise this too will do what other imposed technology has done: the exact opposite of what it purports to do.

The Internet will be a more colourful, exotic place for us with women like Venkatavva flashing their gold nose pins, but what good will it do them? As it is at present, the Internet reflects the perceptions of Northern society that Southern women are brown, backward, and ignorant. A alternative, kinder, depiction of them which is also widespread is that they are victims of their cultural heritage. Is being exposed to such images of themselves going to help Southern women by encouraging them to fight in dignity and self-respect, or will it further erode their confidence in their fast-changing environment?

What, then, is the process by which a woman like Venkatavva could be empowered by the Internet?

Radhika:

Venkatavva should be free to decide how the Internet and other related technologies might be used to benefit and empower her and her community. The tools and access should be provided unconditionally, not as a way of selling a so-called superior life-style modelled on the 'civilised' and urban centres of the world. Women like Ventakavva are perfectly capable of making the decisions needed to empower themselves according to their everyday needs. Policies designed to be empowering should aid and enable, not impose and preach while fostering further inequalities and inadequacies.

I would like to paraphrase (not without reservations similar to those voiced by Annapurna in her rejoinder) a contribution made to the Gender and Law thematic group[10] at the World Bank. For Spivak, the speaker, the key question that emerges in the context of her work with women in Bangladesh is 'How do we approach the bottom?'. That is, 'How can we learn from below?'. The idea is to enter into a society and learn its traditions from inside, seeing what traditions can be worked with to slowly improve the situation, and to ensure that new developments are initiated from the inside so that the changes are accepted. Spivak sees a need to do 'invisible mending' of the native fabric, by weaving in the different positive threads which exist in the fabric (moderatorgl@worldbank.org, 20 April 1999).

Annapurna:

How do we resolve the contradictory sentiments of seeing the Internet as a panacea to the problems of the south; of thinking that on the contrary, it may even be bad for us; and of asserting that this doesn't mean we don't want it? We need to study processes of empowerment and work out how it is to be done in the context of the Internet. While case studies abound for the failure of this process, development workers in particular would not regard it as fair (or politically correct) to down-play the potential of the Internet to empower many women like Venkatavva in South and North. We cannot say, 'I won't give you the Internet, for your own good'.

Radhika:

My experience of observing the development of the Internet, and using this mode of communication, is that while there are hierarchies of power embedded in the very construction and design of Internet culture, there is still potential for using it in ways which might subvert these and foster dialogue and action on various unexpected fronts, in unpredictable ways. However, it remains true that the NGOs who speak with and for women living in poverty throughout the world, as well as the women themselves, have to negotiate and engage in dialogue with the powerful in the North from positions of lesser power. This situation of unequal economic and social power relations between the North and the South presents challenges for people such as myself who are trying to design electronic spaces of dialogue and activism.

Therefore I reiterate the questions central to our discussion in this article, and ask readers to think deeply and honestly about the issues they raise, beyond those we have addressed here. Will women all over the world be able (allowed) to use technologies under conditions that are defined by them, and therefore potentially empowering to them? Within which Internet-based contexts will women of lesser material and cultural privilege within 'global' power relations be able to develop collaborative work, and coalitions, to transform social, cultural, and political structures?

These questions cannot be addressed only in relation to women of the third world. Women from the first world need answers to these questions too. The Internet has its 'headquarters' in the first world, but this does not mean that it is contextually empowering to all women in that context. Whether located in the Northern hemisphere or the South, whether rich or poor, global structures of power (through their 'invisible' control of the market, Internet service providers, software design, language and so on) clearly determine women's use of the Internet. If cyberfeminists want to ensure that the Internet is empowering, it is not enough to 'get connected' and set up websites and maintain e-mail-discussion lists. The latter tasks, while necessary, are only a miniscule part of the battle.

Radhika Gajjala is an Assistant Professor in the Department of Interpersonal Communication, School of Communication Studies, Bowling Green State University, Bowling Green, Ohio, USA. E-mail: radhik@bgnet.bgsu.edu, or cyberdiva16@hotmail.com. Web site: http://ernie.bgsu.edu/~radhik

Annapurna Mamidipudi is a Field Worker, Dastkar Andhra, Secunderabad, India. E-mail: annapurnam@yahoo.com

Notes

1 The writers thank Dr. Melissa Spirek, Dr. A Venkatesh, and the editor of *Gender and Development*, Caroline Sweetman, for commenting on several drafts of this article. Radhika Gajjala also wishes to thank all the Spoon Collective members as well as the members of the various lists that she (co-)moderates. They contribute significantly to our understanding of on-line existence. Several 'real-life' bodies also commented on this article, including family members of both writers.

2 The Internet is a world-wide network of computers which communicate via an agreed set of Internet protocol. The world-wide web is a subset of the Inter-net which uses a combination of text, graphics, audio and video material to provide information on many subjects.

3 I use this term to denote 'the rapidly developing process of complex inter-connections between societies, cultures, institutions and individuals worldwide. It is a process which involves ... shrinking distances through a dramatic reduction in the time taken — either physically or representationally — to cross them, so making the world smaller and in a certain sense bringing human beings 'closer' to one another. But it is also a process which 'stretches' social relations, removing the relationships which govern our everyday lives from local contexts to global ones' (Tomlinson 1997).

4 The term 'on-line' refers to activities carried out via the Internet or e-mail.

5 Getting 'connected' means acquiring the necessary technology (computer, Internet browsing software, telephone modem, connection to an Internet Service Provider) to access the Internet.

6 Even as we collaborate on projects such as this article, we are exchanging non-traditional creative writing, in relation to our personal/ professional/ political conflicts and dilemmas, on sa-cyborgs. For information on sa-cyborgs and third-world women, see http://lists.village.virginia.edu

7 Electronic networks whose participants discuss a particular topic or topics.

8 See http://ernie.bgsu.edu/~radhik

9 The Spoon Collective is operated through the Institute for Advanced Technology in the Humanities at the University of Virginia.

10 Quoted from a post to the gender-law discussion list, gender-law@jazz.world bank.org, received on 29 April 1999.

References

Said, E (1978) *Orientalism*, Pantheon Books, New York.

Tomlinson, J (1997) *'Cultural globalisation and cultural imperialism'* in Mohammadi, A (1997) International Communication and Globalisation, Sage, London.

Uzramma (1995) *'Cotton handlooms -industry of the future'*, paper presented at a seminar on Indian textiles in 1995.

Vitanza, V (1999) *Cyberreader*, Allyn and Bacon, Boston.

Supporting the invisible technologists: The Intermediate Technology Development Group

Maggie Foster

What constitutes 'technology', and who can be described as a technologist? In trying to answer this, the ITDG has uncovered the role of women in areas of production previously considered 'male'. They now try to bridge the gulf between development professionals and poor producers.

The nature of poverty is complex: it is the result of a series of power relationships which affect our whole lives, even our chance of life itself. Perhaps the most important of these relationships in terms of our opportunities for a fully productive life is that which all societies define between the sexes. Development interventions which aim to promote poor people's access to technological support in order to relieve drudgery all too often end up benefiting the better off and the more powerful — who are usually men (Appleton and Scott 1994). Drawing on the experience of the Intermediate Technology Development Group (ITDG), this article argues that technology transfer must be a two-way process, recognising the uniqueness and complexity of the lives of people living in poverty, and the skills and knowledge that they have developed to cope. It must allow those women and men who seek support from development interventions to define their own needs, and to participate in the design and transfer of technology through a dialogue between poor people and project staff. Further, the women and men who live in poverty must retain sufficient control to ensure that an intervention fulfils its objective from their point of view.

ITDG is an international NGO founded in 1966 by the economist Fritz Schumacher, author of *Small is Beautiful: A study of economics as if people mattered* (1973). The organisation is now working from seven self-managing country offices, in Bangladesh, Sri Lanka and Nepal in Asia, Kenya, Sudan and Zimbabwe in Africa, and Peru in Latin America, in addition to its head office in the UK. Since the 1970s, ITDG has been working at improving its own, and others', recognition of the part played by poor people in technology and technological innovation. People's understanding of appropriate technology (AT) and the role of AT organisations has altered over the last 33 years: 'this shift has been primarily towards giving due emphasis to the technological capabilities of people rather than just the characteristics of technologies. The work of IT (and other AT organisations) is therefore now as much about enabling disadvantaged people to identify and develop technologies to address their needs, as these needs change over time, as it is about identifying or developing specific technological options for specific locations at a particular time' (Scott 1996, 4).

This article charts the evolution of ITDG's approaches to gender and technology, and the discovery of poor women 'invisible technologists'. I also focus on our current work with women in industries and sectors traditionally thought to be closed to women, and on the ongoing development of a training tool which aims to bridge the gulf between development professionals and poor producers.

ITDG, GAD and understandings of technology

The prevailing western traditions of technology — even 'appropriate' technology, defined by Schumacher as simple, small-scale, low-cost, and non-violent (Schumacher 1973) — are rooted in a male-dominated culture. Technology has been associated with machines, with hardware located outside the home, with engineering, with men. During the 1970s when ITDG began its project work with communities, the artisans with whom western male experts worked were invariably, although often unconsciously, imagined to be male. This undoubtedly hampered AT organisations from arriving at a useful definition of what constitutes technology, and who the poor producers — the proposed target population for their projects — actually are. It has also made it particularly difficult for ITDG, as an organisation working exclusively in developing-country contexts, to integrate a gender perspective into its work; and yet this is critical if it is to fulfil its aim of effectively targeting the poorest people.

Conducting and recording research carried out since the early 1970s for ITDG, Marilyn Carr considered 50 case studies in 22 poor countries of women involved in 38 unconventional projects which aimed to boost their earning power. The outcome of this work was her book *Blacksmith, Baker, Roofing-sheet Maker* (1984). As the title suggests, Carr found women engaged in light engineering work, as well as work more commonly associated with women. She emphasised the importance of considering women's involvement with technology in a broad context of production and commercial activity, and moving beyond this context to give attention to women's access to credit, raw materials, and markets where their enterprises stood a fair chance of success. In order to promote these ends, she suggested promoting linkages between women's groups, to ensure that the women retain control at all stages of the production process (Carr 1984). This work was conducted in liaison with the Commonwealth Secretariat's Women and Development Programme.

Both within ITDG and outside, under-standings of the key role that technology plays in economic development have become more sophisticated as a result of such research and analysis by both academics and practitioners. It is now clear that technology is concerned with so much more than simply making machines work: it includes not only the hardware or product, but an appreciation of the skills and knowledge, as well as the social organisation, which are necessary for sustaining and adapting technologies in the face of changing circumstances. 'The four Schumacherian characteristics which defined AT and which helped to decide questions of the choice of technology, have given way to a view of technology as one element in a dynamic socio-economic system. Technology is now perceived as having four inter-related constituents: technique, knowledge, organisation and product.' (Scott 1996, 2)

As views of the role of technology in development have evolved, so too has a growing awareness and respect for the technologists living in poverty in developing countries — so many of them women. In the 1980s and early 1990s, ITDG embarked on the 'Tinker, Tiller, Technical Change' project, discussed in the next section, and, later, on the 'Do It Herself' research programme. These programmes worked with local researchers in Africa, Asia, and Latin America to explore the role of poor women and men in technology (Appleton 1995).

Identifying the invisible technologists

The 'Tinker, Tiller, Technical Change' project was the result of case-study work planned and executed by 17 researchers from the 14 countries represented. Each researcher selected a technology in common use in their own country, and carried out detailed field studies of its evolution, its socio-economic importance, and its limitations. The researchers then collaborated with colleagues from their region to identify common issues to consider in more extensive field studies. They shared this work at a seminar in London in 1989. The resulting book (Gamser 1990) was thus a product of both field work and discussion.

Although not primarily focusing on women, the study was alert to the links between gender roles and technological change. 'In all cases, the various activities of the technologies considered were traditionally carried out by women. However, it was observed in each case that, as the technology evolved, the role of women changed. They ceased to be operators and became merely users of the technology. This was observed in all cases but was more vivid where mechanisation was introduced.' (Gamser 1990, 4). Many researchers also noted for the first time the subtle relationship between the producers of technologies (often assumed to be male) and the user (usually a woman). 'The interaction between users and makers of the products under study provided a major

impetus for the development, adaptation, and diffusion of the technologies. Such an interaction continuously transmitted users' experience to the fabricators.' (Gamser 1990, 100). In the course of the debates which took place as a part of the research, the distinction between producers and users became increasingly unclear: suddenly, women were appearing as innovative technologists, previously unrecognised and therefore 'invisible'.

The research confirmed to ITDG that women not only constituted the majority among those living in economic poverty, but that many micro-enterprise producers, and most agro-processors, are women. In the studies, there was a shift away from the view of an end-user of technology being a male artisan working in a small workshop, towards the view of a woman or a family enterprise based within the home. There was, inevitably, another shift away from the concept of technology as complicated machinery, towards the realisation that women, in their everyday work to support their families, use myriad technologies concerned with food production and processing, with fuel economies and provision, animal husbandry, horticulture, with nursing, medicine, child-care, house construction, and many others. For example, women in Sudan carry out extremely complex fermentation processes using little more than gourds and knives (Dirar in Appleton and Scott 1994). 'Recognition of the value of peoples' technology is the necessary first step towards strengthening this technology, and organisations behind it … At the same time, support for people's technology has to respect the informality under which it thrives' (Gamser 1990, xvi).

As the research progressed, and the value of women's contribution to technology became clearer, it became obvious that the implicit undervaluing of women's skills, knowledge, and organisation of technology must have serious implications for their involvement in processes of technology development. 'Traditional models of technology development may fail women simply because they do not address the differences between men's and women's technological needs, uses and contributions' (Appleton and Scott 1994, 1). This finding is echoed in an example of a research programme in Peru, which aimed to document local knowledge of livestock diseases. Researchers contacted male heads of households, only to discover that men knew little about the subject. When researchers questioned the women, the true extent of local knowledge of livestock was revealed (Appleton and Scott 1994).

'Do It Herself': Investigating women and technical innovation

The 'Do It Herself' research programme, which culminated in an exhibition, conference, and book of the same name (Appleton 1995) was designed to investigate the contributions of women to technical innovation at grassroots level. The research programme started from the assumption that women in developing countries have specialist technical knowledge, and looked at how they use their technical knowledge and skills to develop, modify, and adapt the techniques and technical processes with which they work.

'A major challenge for the research was to be the obtaining of information about an area — women and technological innovation at local level — that was to some extent invisible, and therefore unlikely to be easily accessed by conventional research methodologies' (Appleton 1995, 3). The solution to the methodological quandary about how to see the invisible was solved by involving the users in the research, thereby creating an opportunity for them to express their views. Researchers with good community links were identified, and support offered to strengthening regional capacity with regard to women's contributions to technical innovation.

As a result of this research work, and the parallel evolution of participatory technology development (PTD) concepts within AT organisations, evidence was collected that strongly suggested that ITDG and its partner organisations had made progress over the past seven years in developing a participatory approach to technological development; in recognition of women's important role in food production and agro-processing, we had worked in close consultation with host communities.

Discovering the invisible engineers

ITDG's experience to date challenges the idea that traditional producers are resistant to change. Although technical change is the result of a complex interaction between processes of technical design, and a society's ways of interacting and making decisions, small-scale producers make rational choices based on their own perception of their needs, and the resources available to them (Gamser 1990). Such an understanding of the ways in which producers adapt to changing situations through technological change is a firm basis on which to develop technology interventions in ways that reflect local skills, priorities and needs. It has been an important consideration in the design for many ITDG projects, including the Sri Lanka Forum on Rural Transport Development, and projects focusing on food-processing for income generation in Bangladesh, small enterprise promotion in Bangladesh, and dissemination of building-materials technologies in Zimbabwe.

It is becoming clear that women are increasingly tackling productive work not only in sectors associated with 'women's skills', and their traditional domestic role. Against all odds, they are endeavouring, out of necessity, to compete with men in more traditional engineering tasks. Marilyn Carr recognised the existence of such women producers in 1984, but according to her findings they were few in number. Today, it appears that there are still relatively few, but we now know that our increasing awareness of them is not only due to their numbers. Our preconceptions, and problems in finding an appropriate research methodology, may have obscured the true extent of women doing jobs of this nature, many of whom see themselves as 'helping out' within family businesses. In a recent report, Kusala Weththasinghe of IT Sri Lanka reported a 'small but significant involvement of women in [light engineering], a sector that most of us believed to be "closed" to women ... The project really aimed to involve women by helping small-scale artisans to consider women's needs when designing and making tools and equipment. Now, at the initial stages we see two types of involvement by women. One is supporting the business by maintaining financial records. The other is actually being involved in the production' (internal report, 1999).

The women who assist and support their male relatives within such family enterprises by using business skills, keeping books or doing the marketing are involved in a powerful function in traditionally male-dominated sectors 'through the back door'. An avenue for research is how the status of the women responsible for the financial viability of their businesses rises in their family and their community. In addition to playing this role, these women, their daughters or others who have watched them, may feel able in the future to attend engineering training to enable them to participate as engineers in the business, either alongside male relatives or in their stead. In the IT internal report, Kusala Weththasinghe stated: 'In a village where the project is promoting a collective effort to help a cluster of very poor blacksmith families, we have met a woman who is involved in the production side by side with her husband. She says she learned the

craft as a school girl. Her brother was a blacksmith and she took time off from her studies to work with him. In the black-smithing sector women may be collecting coconuts, burning them to prepare charcoal, cleaning up the workshop, helping pull the blower (most blacksmiths still use a traditional blower) etc. but the share of their contribution is not recognised even by themselves ... if I ask outright what they do at the workshop, they promptly reply "Oh. It is my husband (son/brother) who does that work. I cannot do these things".' Kusala Weththasinghe believes that the perception of women's role in light engineering by communities and by project workers is similar to that of the agricultural sector some years ago: 'It is generally assumed that only men are involved in the production. The work done by women is invisible because it is seen as "help". The fact that most small-scale light engineering workshops are located in part of the house is another reason why the contribution of the women may not be noticed' (ibid.).

Kusala Weththasinghe reports being informed by a partner organisation about a woman welder in Hambantota, south Sri Lanka, who took up the job after the death of her husband: 'The lady has learned the craft because she had no other way to support her children. She cannot use any helpers in the workshop because the society frowns upon men spending time in a house where a man does not live! For the same reason she is reluctant to go for training to develop her skills'(ibid.). The partner organisation is currently trying to arrange for an experienced craftsman to visit her workshop and train her. They will make sure that some of their women community development workers are present while the training is conducted.

Another example of women engineers comes from Bangladesh. Significantly for organisations who are committed to promoting a change in gender power relations, Mahjabeen Mukib in IT Bangladesh reports unexpected support from the community towards women are involved in engineering in a project supported by ITDG. In her view, 'to consider women only as consumers of the sector leads to the fallacy of sustaining the perception of outsiders (us) who assume that women cannot be employed in light engineering. Small interventions through our project will not increase women's participation in the sector immensely but will dispel the myth of this sector being a 'male domain'. It is necessary to set up examples in order to boost women's self-confidence and position in society vis-à-vis men. This is also in an attempt to increase life's options ... We went with an open mind and were surprised to find out that we (as outsiders) have more resistance within ourselves and in our attitudes as opposed to those who are a part of the sector or who have links with the light engineering sector ... There is enough support and willingness on the part of the community members to the idea of women's involvement in light engineering activity but there is still a lot to be done ...' (internal report, 1999).

Current challenges

Promoting learning among 'outsiders'

Growing awareness of the issues faced by women technologists has focused attention not only on the methods used to communicate with them, but on the skills and training needed by field workers and project staff to equip them to work in co-operation with the women. ITDG 'is aware that addressing gender relations is usually the most difficult aspect of project implementation' (IT Kenya Gender Impact Assessment Study Report for the Pastoralist Project, Luta Shaba 1999, 6). It is a great challenge to understand the gendered nature of poverty, of productive and reproductive survival strategies, of what women actually do and how outside intervention

affects their jobs and benefits. Both these reports highlight the fact that much more awareness is needed from us as 'outsiders', and that our assumptions about the productive activities of poor women must be continuously questioned. A 'large amount of skill and knowledge may exist within a community, but much of this is not recognised by outsiders. Even where it is recognised, local people may not have the self-confidence to draw upon this store of experience and see ways in which it can be used as the basis for understanding and using a "new" level of technology. This means that when outsiders work alongside rural people they have to be able to bring an holistic viewpoint with them, rather than one constrained by the boundaries of an academic discipline' (Appleton and Croxton 1994, 3).

'Mainstreaming' gender in a technical organisation

ITDG faces the particular challenge that it has always been an organisation for promoting the transfer of appropriate technology, but that technology itself is a concept imbued with male bias. However, it is not an organisation made up of 'technologists' alone. It aims to draw on the skills of both social scientists and technologists, and not to create an artificial divide between these two disciplines. Increasingly, ITDG technicians are moving towards listening, learning, and facilitating development in partnership with the communities they serve. ITDG does not have gender project officers as such; in fact, we are against the idea, preferring to 'mainstream gender' by expecting all project staff to take responsibility for including a gender perspective in projects.

Recognising development as a gradual process

The time-scale against which development practitioners measure change is important for those projects which confront deep-rooted attitudes involving gender roles and responsibilities. In these interventions, there is a challenge to maintain accountability while at the same time being ready to take risks, to follow tentative leads, and to await gradual transformations with patience. The current emphasis in many NGOs on short-term impact measurement may obscure more important long-term issues. This appreciation of slow change over time is very much part of the participatory approach to community energy development in ITDG-supported interventions in Zimbabwe and Mozambique. In Nepal, reports on IT's support to the micro-hydro sector talk of small beginnings, of 'a small step forward'. In Bangladesh the small enterprise unit talks of 'gradually moving towards a gender-sensitive direction.' (internal reports, 1999) Sometimes the most valuable impacts are slow-maturing, unexpected, and difficult to measure. You cannot quickly build peer respect, foster self-confidence, or have an impact through a solitary role model. Attitudinal change can take a generation.

Developing a tool to meet these challenges

In the face of these challenges, there is a growing awareness that information and training are required, to help those working directly with poor women and men technologists understand how gender differences underpin the acquisition and use of technical skills, and also examine the social status given to different technical tasks performed by women and men. We also need to revolutionise the way information about these technologists and their knowledge and skills is communicated between poor communities. 'The possibility of local people, especially women, being able to contribute to courses, and to assess, modify, adapt and innovate technologies themselves, was formerly not considered and did not form part of the thinking behind training design. As a result, such courses, because they 'talk at' rather than 'work

with' producers, fail to build or strengthen existing technical innovation skills among women and men, and have a particularly limited impact on women, whose domestic roles render them less visible.' (internal draft training manual, 1998). Training courses such as these may have actually reduced the confidence and status of women as producers.

ITDG has been developing an improved training method with a manual entitled 'Discovering Technologists: Women's and men's work at village level' (unpublished, 1998). Videos, slides, cartoon illustrations, posters, and a manual are included in the training pack. This manual is intended to be a tool which can be used in every project, to help highlight the existing technical capacity of poor women and men, and to show that this is flexible and adaptable. It should assist partner NGO field staff to communicate more effectively with the people involved in projects, and quickly disseminate the information gathered during the training (with the permission of participants). The modules are participatory, and include the opportunity for debate and involvement in technology development. They also explore ways of designing the project which will minimise the danger that benefits will be appropriated by the better-off. In short, the training endeavours to involve local people in the development, acknowledgement and dissemination of local technical capacity.

The training method was tested by local NGOs in Sri Lanka, and subsequently tested and discussed by ITDG gender and technology co-ordinators who participated in a workshop in Sri Lanka in January 1999. Two people responsible for co-ordinating the pilot training from each country where ITDG works attended; staff in the Sri Lanka, Bangladesh and Zimbabwe offices are particularly enthusiastic and committed. Currently, the manual is being further pilot-tested; training has already been held for participants from local NGOs in Kenya and in Zimbabwe, using funds made available through Comic Relief. Funding is currently being sought for the workshop to be held in Sri Lanka, Bangladesh, Peru, Sudan, and Nepal. A copy of the training pack — which includes the exhibition resources from the Do It Herself research, the video, slides, posters, and books of illustrations for illiterate participants — is issued to each participant at the end of the workshop. Since the Sri Lanka workshop, ITDG has been able to draw on the views of a very active international 'team' who continue to share experiences on integrating gender issues into their work. It is encouraging that this team is not made up only of social scientists, or only of women, but in fact includes women and men technicians, communications specialists, and social scientists.

Maggie Foster is Gender and Technology Specialist at ITDG, Schumacher Centre for Technology and Development, Burton Hall, Burton on Dunsmore, Rugby CV23 9QZ, UK. Fax: +44 (0)1788 661 101. E-mail: maggief@itdg.org.uk

References

Appleton, H (1995) *Do It Herself: Women and technical innovation*, IT Publications, London.

Appleton, H and Scott, A (1994) 'Gender issues in agricultural technology', development paper presented at a workshop for agricultural engineers for FAO, 1994.

Croxton, S and Appleton, H (1994) 'The role of participative approaches in increasing the technical capacity and technology choice of rural communities', paper presented at a workshop on Technology for Rural Livelihoods: Current Issues for Engineers and Social Scientists, September 1994.

Gamser, MS, Appleton, H, Carter, N (1990) *Tinker, Tiller, Technical Change*, IT Publications, London.

Schumacher, Fritz (1974) *Small Is Beautiful: A study of economics as though people mattered*, Abacus Edition, Sphere Books Ltd.

Scott, A (1996) *Appropriate Technology*, Vol.23, No.3, pp.1-4.

Marketing treadle pumps to women farmers in India

Maya Prabhu[1]

International Development Enterprises India (IDE) endeavours to provide both women and men farmers with access to knowledge about the technologies it promotes, and about the income-earning opportunities that arise from participating in the delivery of these technologies. Maya Prabhu discusses how the organisation has tried to define and integrate gender awareness into its thinking and internal practices as well as its programme of technology dissemination.

Until a few years ago, advocates of the use of appropriate technology for development tended to overlook or misrepresent women's circumstances and needs, even though a key aspect of developing appropriate technology is to answer the question: 'appropriate for whom?' It is now widely recognised by development theorists and policy-makers that not only is technology not gender-neutral, but it can also be a tool to change gender relations. Through using technology, women can gain a chance of empowerment: their daily lives can be made easier, and they can challenge the stereotypical gender roles, through gaining time, skills, and knowledge to participate in other kinds of work. In particular, women's use of new technologies in non-traditional spheres such as in the commercial farm sector potentially challenges the rigid traditional polarisation of tasks as 'men's' and 'women's'.

IDE's approach

Initiated by a group of North American entrepreneurs in 1981, International Development Enterprises (IDE) is an inter-national not-for-profit organisation with headquarters in Denver, USA. IDE's work is currently funded by the Swiss Agency for Development and Cooperation, the Interchurch Organisation for Development Cooperation, Misereor, the United States Agency for International Development, and the Dutch Government. Working in Asia and Africa, IDE aims to improve the lives of the world's poorest people through its twin goals of developing and disseminating simple, low-cost, and appropriate technologies, and stimulating local enterprise to deliver these technologies on a for-profit basis. IDE technologies must fulfil the organisation's requirements by being affordable, easy to maintain, and capable of producing a net rate of return of at least 100 per cent per year for the user farmer.

There are two basic means of promoting appropriate technology: the first is by using trained extension workers. The major advantage of this is that it provides a free service to the poorest farmers. Yet its disadvantage is that government and non-government organisations can never fund enough extension agents (at least in India) to reach the scores of people who need, and will benefit from, using the technology. A further disadvantage for women farmers and those who aim to improve gender power relations is that extension agents in India are mostly men[2], who for cultural reasons tend to restrict their interactions to male farmers, assuming that no woman would be interested in irrigation technology.

The other route is to promote technology through the private sector. The advantages of this route are obvious: it harnesses the efficiencies of the private sector to promote and supply technologies on a large scale. IDE believes that its success stems from its treatment of poor people as customers and not recipients of charity, and the fact that it disseminates products that are affordable and appropriate for their needs.

In India, IDE promotes treadle pumps (a foot-operated water lifting device) in selected districts of Uttar Pradesh, Bihar, West Bengal, Assam, Meghalaya, and Orissa. Over the past four years, IDE has also test-marketed a second major product — affordable micro-irrigation systems (drip and sprinkler systems) — in India and Nepal, and these technologies have met with a similar positive response. IDE has just begun scaling up the promotion of affordable micro-irrigation technology in several semi-arid regions of India including Rajasthan, Gujarat, Madhya Pradesh, Maharashtra, Karnataka, Andhra Pradesh, and Himachal Pradesh.

Since IDE started working in the region in the late 1980s, small and marginal farmers in south Asia (who cultivate less than one acre of land usually divided into several plots) have purchased over 1.4 million treadle pumps to irrigate their land, through over 3,000 small enterprises (local hardware and agriculture input shops). These pumps are mostly bought by male farmers, but used both by male and female farmers. Treadle pumps are used extensively by women, particularly in areas where male migration rates are high.

From IDE's internal sales records, we estimate that 95 per cent of treadle-pumps are bought by male-headed households. However, this data may be misleading, as in-house qualitative studies reveal many instances of women buying the pump but asking for their son or other male relative's name to be written on the purchaser's warranty card. This card (which the local dealer fills in) is the primary means for us to track the number of pumps sold and, more importantly, to receive information on who buys them. Information from a short gender-analysis study[3] which I conducted for IDE in 1998 showed that, while women may not make actual purchases, they strongly influence the decision to purchase this product.

Working with NGOs and the private sector

Building supply networks

IDE aims for a broad impact through a comprehensive strategy of creating awareness about technologies, thus increasing demand for them, and at the same time ensuring their availability (supply). This strategy is put into place in several districts within a state. In building the supply network for appropriate technologies, IDE works with and through others, creating linkages between and building on the strengths of the private sector and NGOs. Because private businesses must make a profit, they have a strong incentive to deliver products in a sustainable manner. NGOs, for their part, often enjoy strong relationships of trust and respect with their target group. This relationship helps in the introduction of a new technology or idea. NGOs are also a critical link because they can offer the poorest farmers credit to purchase the product.

IDE works in partnership with the local private sector through identifying and motivating suitable manufacturers to make the product, linking them with appropriate distributors and dealers who will stock and supply the product at the grassroots level, and training local mechanics to provide after-sales service (see graph below). Each of the private-sector players in the supply chain is self-sustaining, as they operate on a for-profit basis. IDE offers support to them by building their capacity to manage business operations, monitor quality control, and by aggressively promoting the products in rural areas. We employ innovative tools of rural marketing (much like a private-sector company would). These tools are described further on in this paper.

Local NGOs play an important role as IDE's other partners: they stock products, help create awareness about them among their target group, and assist in providing training to mechanics and farmers . They also provide farmers with credit, if necessary[4]. IDE itself aims only to build the links between the private sector and NGOs to enable them to distribute appropriate technologies to marginalised people.

Rural marketing

IDE uses innovative methods of rural marketing to promote technology among farmers. These include highly interactive farmers' meetings; product demonstrations, for example at village bazaars and fairs; and video shows of a hugely entertaining commercial film (with the necessary ingredient of melodrama!) whose action is centred around the treadle pump. All these promotional techniques are employed to varying degree in each area, depending on the level of awareness about the product.

Farmers' meetings constitute IDE's most important point of contact with farmers; in the areas where treadle pumps have been promoted alone, IDE conducts over 8,000 farmers' meetings each year, reaching out to over 160,000 farmers. These meetings last between 45 minutes and one hour, and are attended by groups of 15-20 farmers. The meetings are not only a means for IDE to promote the treadle pump, but also serve to provide farmers with tips on improved agricultural practices. The treadle pump is not a 'community product' (one which lends itself to community ownership and management), and IDE therefore works directly with individual farm families; but community-level promotion efforts such as farmers' meetings enable us to understand the needs and aspirations of marginalised farmers as a social grouping. Ideas for new products come out of these meetings and

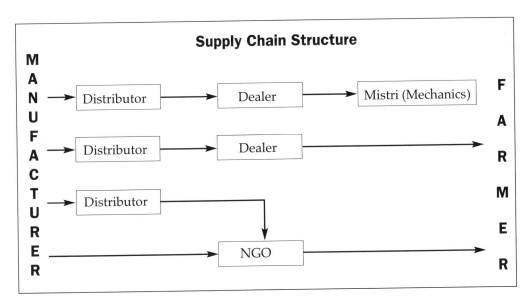

Supply Chain Structure

other forms of direct contact. IDE staff follow up farmers' meetings with visits to existing users of treadle pumps in order to check on the quality of installations, to train them in regular maintenance of the pumps, and to ensure that they have access to a mechanic for repairs, should the need arise. These one-on-one meetings are also used to gauge the farmers' satisfaction with the product. All this feedback is channelled back into IDE.

Gender, technology, and marketing

The process of mainstreaming gender concerns into IDE's work here in India began about two years ago, across several states in the country[5]. Since 1997, external evaluators and funders have advised IDE to empower rural women by targeting them as purchasers and users of our products, and by training them to maintain and repair them. Sulagna Sengupta, a consultant who assessed the impact of the treadle pump for IDE, mentions that there are 'widespread phenomena of women treadling the pump in marginal and small farmer households who are mostly from scheduled (backward) castes' (internal report, 1999). Internal data on the profile of treadle-pump users as well as external studies showed that the extent to which women use the treadle pump differs from state to state and from community to community[6], but that overall the treadle pump is used by many women.

In 1987-88, 85 per cent of rural female workers and 75 per cent of rural male workers in India were employed in agriculture (Govt. of India, quoted in Agarwal 1994), demonstrating the contribution of women to Indian agriculture. Women are traditionally responsible for kitchen gardens, while the main fields tend to be men's responsibility. However, the men of many households using treadle pumps have taken to supplementing the family

income by working on a richer farmer's land, or through off-farm labour. Especially in these cases, the women of the household perform all agricultural tasks from sowing and weeding to harvesting, with the single exception of ploughing. Women from backward castes and tribes in India particularly contribute to farming operations, including irrigation by treadle pumps.

Among the women managing farms who Sengupta met during the course of her research for IDE was a woman aged about 45, who ran the farm with help from her children and daughter-in-law, while her husband attended to his shop in the local market. Her son helped with powering the pump by pedalling from time to time, while her daughter-in-law was responsible for domestic chores. Sengupta's research shows that little effort was made to consult this woman, or others, in the design process, to understand the impact of the treadle pump on their lives, or indeed to view them as potential 'customers'.

For an organisation such as IDE, it is immensely challenging to acknowledge women as users of technology, and to adapt our working practices according to their needs. Thinking of women as 'customers' for the technologies means ridding our work of predominantly masculine values, which is hard because most of IDE's marketing staff are young men[7]. Consider the machismo associated with achieving sales targets or well-defined quantitative indicators, and you realise that little space is left for 'gender' concerns and the development of 'softer', more qualitative indicators of success.

Advertising and marketing

Adopting a commercial route involves promoting technologies through various means of advertising, and these usually conform to gender stereotypes. Like extension agents, advertising managers and sales representatives in the commercial sector are mostly men. Many bring 'traditional' perspectives about 'men's' and 'women's' worlds to their work. For instance, if an organisation wishes to advertise an improved cooking stove, it will target women in their publicity campaigns, which makes sense in terms of the current gender division of labour. However, in the area of agriculture, advertising and sales activities almost exclusively target men, as it is often seen, falsely, as a male-only domain. Advertising or promotional campaigns that do aim to reach both men and women purchasers to promote different kinds of products can be a powerful means of breaking some gender stereotypes. Incorporating a gender perspective into promotional campaigns has implications for the type of media chosen, and the contents of the message.

Advertisers who aim to deliver a message to women face challenges such as relatively low literacy levels[8], and restricted opportunities for displaying or delivering your message. If you wanted to advertise an improved seed for potatoes to both men and women (using, say, a poster), you would praise the benefits of the seed through pictures rather than heavy copy, and put it up at places where men and women congregate. For men, this might be the local cigarette shop, for women the local bangle and sari shop. In addition, you would place the advertisement at the shop selling the seeds. A major obstacle faced by advertisers in rural India is the relatively low mobility level of women outside their homes or their villages.

Designing appropriate supply strategies

Gender differences also affect supply strategies. Going back to the seed example, women usually do not visit shops that sell agricultural goods such as seeds and fertilisers. If you would want women to be able to buy this product (and as they commonly manage their households' vegetable gardens, even if they are not involved in other agricultural activities, they would be

a natural customer group) you would have to find an alternative outlet, preferably village-based, such as a commission agent or the village grocery store.

The impact of the treadle pump on gender relations

IDE has commissioned a wider independent study to analyse how using the treadle pump has affected intra-household dynamics between women and men in India, Nepal, and Bangladesh. The report (available from IDE by the end of 1999) looks at women's and men's participation in, and organisation of, work, changes in occupation and employment, earning potential, and so on. In this section, I will focus on the impact of marketing treadle pumps to women farmers in the district of Sitamarhi in north Bihar, India.

The socio-cultural landscape of Sitamarhi district is strongly patriarchal and feudal. Agriculture is the major source of livelihoods; small and marginal farmers[9] predominate. While this district is blessed with fertile land and abundant ground-water resources, marginal farmers face continual challenges in improving the productivity of their land, which for the most part requires that they have assured access to water. Women (particularly those from disadvantaged caste and class backgrounds) play an important role in agriculture. They do not plough, but are involved — and often play a key role in — all other aspects of farming, partly because male migration rates from the district are high (personal observation and communications, 1998-89). Before IDE began promoting the treadle pump in the area, women (belonging predominantly to the vegetable-growing castes of kushwahas or kurmis) used hand-pumps up to six hours per day in order to irrigate the family's small vegetable plots. A high proportion of the men in the area migrated to cities and towns in search of work, or worked as farm labourers, as the lack of assured access to irrigation rendered their fields unprofitable (discussions with women, April 1998).

Once IDE introduced treadle pumps in the area — primarily targeting male farmers — the households where male migration had not taken place adopted the treadle pumps, chiefly because it offered them 'water independence' or 'assured access to irrigation' (market research, ORG-MARG, New Delhi, 1999). There was a clear need to provide the women in the households where men were absent with information about, and access to, treadle pumps, both as a means to reduce their workload, and to introduce them to a non-traditional technology.

The first challenge was to provide women with information about this technology, since IDE's staff were predominantly male; the second was to set up supply outlets from which women could purchase the pumps. IDE promotes treadle pumps through the private sector in this district: local hardware shops stock the product, while IDE promotes it through the methods outlined above. Due to socio-cultural factors including *purdah* requirements, women do not normally visit hardware shops. Moreover, they do not view 'hardware' as their domain, so even if they did visit the markets they would not enter a hardware shop to look out for new equipment (discussions with women, 1998).

IDE met these challenges in the following manner. First, it ensured that all IDE field staff made an effort to reach both men and women during promotional events such as farmers' meetings, demonstrations, and video-van shows. It has taken quite a lot of persuasion from our staff (with support from influential women) to persuade women to participate in 'mixed' promotional events. In the local culture, women, particularly young women, do not sit in the presence of the male elders of their families, including their fathers-in-law and older brothers-in-law. Thus, where the

social situation restricted women's participation in the presence of men, we set up separate meetings with women farmers. Second, IDE worked with influential local women and opinion-formers, including local teachers and leaders of self-help groups. The greatest challenge for our male staff (and an on-going one) is how to talk to women without such a gesture being misinterpreted. Seeking out and working with female opinion-leaders greatly helps to overcome this.

Another strategy was to work with local NGOs, including one which has established a network of active women's self-help groups. We also conducted pump demonstrations among women, encouraging them to try the demonstrated technology; and established demonstration plots with women-headed households. Using the demonstration plot, we trained women users in basic pump maintenance and good agricultural practice, particularly in growing vegetables which improve family nutrition and command a good market price. We appointed an enterprising woman (the secretary of the self-help group) in the area as a dealer for treadle pumps, who would be able to earn a steady income from commissions earned off pump sales. Finally, we provided training for local IDE staff (all male) on gender issues, the importance of women farmers as customers and, most importantly, on how to interact with women. Throughout this whole process, we ensured that we consistently talked with the men in the family as well. As a result of these efforts, over 18 months 75 pumps were sold to marginal women farmers with credit support from their groups.

Over the past two years, there has been a perceptible change in the circumstances of women who have begun using treadle pumps (internal report, 1998). All the women say that the time spent on irrigation has been substantially reduced. With this decrease in workload, they have been able to send their children back to school instead of keeping them at home to work in the fields. Most women have begun growing higher-value seasonal vegetables, to bring in income. However, much more needs to be done to train the women in timing their crops in order to get the best price. The women express a strong interest in learning more about agriculture. Initially, many stated that they felt that this was not really their domain, but with consistent effort on our part they began to view themselves as important contributors to cultivation[10].

The men in the family are beginning to make important shifts as well. While initially they were resistant to the idea of their wives and daughters participation in agricultural and technical training, they now see the benefits of the small vegetable gardens for the family, and recognise the women's contribution to growing vegetables in the main plot. Finally, perhaps most importantly for many women, using the treadle pump has meant a major change in their lives, because it has involved them in using machinery. Moreover, it has enabled many them to grow extra vegetables in the main family plot (ibid.).

Our impact on poverty

IDE has often been asked whether it is able to reach the 'poorest of the poor' farmers through its market-based approach. Given the nature of the work we are engaged in (i.e., promoting affordable irrigation systems), we would define the poorest farmers in our target group as those who are termed 'landless' or who only own kitchen gardens. IDE certainly aims to improve the livelihoods of these farmers by providing them with access to irrigation so that they can grow vegetables profitably. We have observed the following pattern for treadle pump adoption in a village: the first pumps are bought by the opinion leaders who are better-off farmers but still fall within the category of marginal and small

farmers[11]. Once other, poorer, farmers in the village have observed the product work and seen its impact on the other farmers' output over at least one or two crop cycles, they invest in it as well. The reason for this is simple: poorer farmers cannot take risks and invest in a product whose returns they are not sure about. In order to reduce the time-lag between the poorest farmers first seeing the product and their eventual purchase, IDE works with local NGOs and the supply chain to provide credit, which absorbs some of the risk. Thus, adopting a more commercial route to promoting technologies does not limit one's ability to reach the poorest. It does, however, mean taking into account from the start the time it will take to reach the poorest farmers. Having said that, I believe that if you have products that are really cheap, you can reach the poorest farmers at the outset. IDE will this year launch products including agricultural implements (corn husker, grubber, and weeder) which cost US$0.5, US$1, and US$6 respectively.

Lessons from IDE's experience

We now know from experience that there is a long learning curve on integrating gender concerns with technology development and dissemination. It is critical to move slowly and strategically, and be prepared to take small steps. It is very important to recognise that each geographical area has its own peculiarities, which must be explored and understood before steps are made in accordance with local conditions.

We have learned, first, that products must be developed with an understanding of gender roles and relations, because the nature of the technology itself will determine the degree to which it is adopted by women. IDE has now built this consideration into its procedures: we have field-tested our low-cost agricultural implements and micro-irrigation kits. We are now ready to sell these products on a large scale; all of them aim to reduce the women's workload.

In marketing terms, we have learned that sales to women are not in themselves a sufficient indicator of the level of involvement of women in the use of the technologies we are promoting. While women may not actually go to shops to buy the technologies, they may significantly influence the decision to purchase, and therefore information about the product should be made available to them. It is important to include other indicators of their involvement in monitoring and evaluation, such as women's attendance at training sessions and promotional events. With this additional information, the nature and degree of women's participation can be judged more accurately.

An important learning point is that if an organisation wants to integrate a gender perspective into its programme, there is no point in having separate staff implementing a 'gender' programme which simply targets women for sales and promotion, which tends to isolate the issue of gender power relations. I strongly believe that being a woman places you in a disadvantageous position to talk about gender in the first place. One of my major aims over the last two years has been to win over male colleagues as allies and indeed to get them to support the importance of integrating gender in IDE — both in the programme, and within the organisation. Without the support of these few key individuals, progress would have been impossible. It is important that all staff see the potential of both men and women as users of technologies, and the potential of using technologies to challenge unequal gender relations.

Integrating gender into recruitment, performance appraisal, and other personnel policies can be very problematic, and lead to resentment among staff. From my experience, it is more expedient — political, if you like — to allow a strong rationale for

the need to integrate gender issues into the programme to emerge, before emphasising that this necessitates change in the organisation itself. We have found that there is no substitute for regular, non-threatening orientation on gender issues for all staff. It is important that this training combines conceptual awareness-building and practical tips for implementation. Another early step that we found useful is to put in writing a brief, lucid policy statement on gender issues in the context of our organisation's work.

Iin a technology-orientated organisation staff tend to expect clear, definite answers on what 'gender' is, and on how they can integrate it into their work. They anticipate ready linear models (preferably with quantitative deliverables) to implement a gender-sensitive programme, and complain of lack of clarity if this is not there. In this context, it is difficult to advocate a more process-orientated and flexible approach. Integrating gender into the development and marketing of appropriate technologies is a relatively new area, and therefore there are few models to emulate. A big challenge for IDE is to develop good qualitative indicators to measure the impact over time of integrating gender issues into our activities. We plan to carry out small action-research projects over the next year to fine-tune our understanding of various aspects of the development and marketing of technologies. IDE is also keen to develop partnerships with other NGOs and funders interested in gender and technology, to share information and evolve common platforms of learning. Another challenge is to increase the commitment of our staff to incorporate a gender-awareness into all our work.

Taken together, these insights have helped clarify IDE's goals on gender work in its programmes. These are to help women own an asset in non-traditional spheres such as agriculture; to save their labour; to help them generate income; and to improve their skills and knowledge in agriculture — a sector to which they make great, but invisible, contributions. From these first four aims, IDE hopes over time to improve women's decision-making status in the household, and to expand their domain into the public sphere. For us at IDE India, this is just a beginning.

Maya Prabhu is Senior Manager for Gender and Development, IDE, C5/43 SDA, New Delhi 110 016, India. Tel: +91 11 696 9812/ 696 9813/ 696 4632. Fax: +91 11 696 5313; e-mail: ide@ideindia.org / mayaprabhurajan@hotmail.com

Notes

1   The author is Senior Manager for Gender and Development at IDE India. The views expressed in this piece are my own.

2   Only 0.5 per cent of extension workers in India in the 1980s were women (ibid.). However, donors like DANIDA have recognised this as a problem and have initiated projects to train women extension workers in Orissa.

3   The gender-analysis study was carried out in 1998 by Maya Prabhu and Sarat Dash. It used qualitative methods such as focus-group discussions and individual interviews with women.

4   Our experience with more formal credit mechanisms such as Regional Rural Banks has not been very successful due to the high transaction cost. We have therefore sought to provide farmers with access to credit through NGO partners and private-sector dealers, if they request it; we do not use 'availability of credit' as a promotion tool.

5   My passionate belief in the importance of an awareness of gender issues to make development interventions more effective led me to champion this agenda within IDE.

6   For example, among higher castes, women may not be permitted to leave the household and therefore do not participate in agricultural work.

7   Sales jobs in rural India typically entail high levels of daily travel over 50-60kms by motorbikes or mopeds. This makes it difficult (though not impossible) to hire local women for these jobs, particularly in more conservative states like Uttar Pradesh and Bihar.

8   It is important to note that challenges such as low literacy facing organisations such as IDE not only spring from gender differences; they also encompass problems which arise from other aspects of social differentiation, such as caste.

9   Those with less than 1 hectare of land.

10   Prof. Tushaar Shah, in *Social Impact of the Treadle Pump Programme: Foundation Study Field Notes (Orissa, 1999)*, writes: '… we met Asalata Parida … she looked a miserable person, divorced barely three months from her husband who has already married another women. Her son died; and a daughter was given to her husband's custody by the Caste Panchayat. Asalata is now dependent on her invalid brother, and has begun to take full responsibility of the farm, including the treadle pump; it looked as though pedalling the treadle pump is going to be her way of living with a modicum of self-respect as a dependent in her brother's family.'

11   The treadle pump in that sense is a self-selecting product largely due to the fact that it is manually operated and is designed for small plots. No 'rich' farmer will be interested in this product.

References

Agarwal, B (1994) *A Field of One's Own: Gender and Land Rights in South Asia*, Cambridge University Press.

Carr, M (1997) *'Gender and technology: Is there a problem?'*, paper prepared for TOOL/TOOL Consult Conference on Technology and Development: Strategies for the Integration of Gender, Amsterdam, 6 June.

Reproductive health technologies and gender:

Is participation the key?

Katie Chapman and Gill Gordon[1]

This article discusses the impact of a community-based distribution (CBD) project in Eastern Province, Zambia, on reproductive health and gender relations. It shows how reproductive health can be furthered through participatory methods, including both 'hard' information technologies and 'soft' communications techniques[2] to promote the use of reproductive technologies in controlling fertility and protecting against sexually transmitted diseases.

For the past 30 years, feminists have sought to answer the question whether reproductive technologies are women's friend or foe. The debates have tended to be polarised. The main criticisms put forward by those arguing that these technologies are unfriendly to women hinge on limitations in the safety, effectiveness, and acceptability of reproductive technologies — in particular, contraceptives. Advocates of women's health have criticised the choice of available contraceptives for not meeting reproductive needs, and for controlling women's fertility at the expense of their health (see Hardon 1994 and 1997). Women's experiences in using the methods, and the impact of such use on their daily lives, including their relationships with men, have often been ignored in the research and development process. Women's health advocates have called for a more comprehensive analysis of context-related effects of the methods, and of the users' perspectives on appropriateness and safety, at an early stage of contraceptive development (Hardon 1994). Accompanying these arguments are those which focus on the potential (or actual) abuse of contraceptive technologies in coercing women to control their fertility (see Hartmann 1987, Dixon-Mueller 1993).

Alternatively, those who see reproductive technologies as beneficial to women, have heralded them as a means for women to control their reproductive role and balance this with other aspects of their lives. In this light, contraceptive technologies have the potential to alter gender roles in families and societies (Schuler, 1998). Evidence of this is provided by various studies from different cultural contexts. For instance, a study from The Gambia shows how contraceptives have the practical benefit of enabling women to rest between successive pregnancies. This break from childbearing is seen as particularly useful for women who have undergone obstetric trauma or reproductive mishaps (Beldsoe, Banja and Hill, 1998). In contrast to this, the potential of family planning and reproductive health[3] programmes for explicitly 'empowering' women has also been emphasised (see Dixon-Mueller 1993, and Population Reports Series M, No. 12, 1994), arguing that contraceptive technologies can promote equality between women and men. Another, related, view focuses on the opportunity these offer some women to enjoy their sexuality without fear of pregnancy (Dixon-Mueller 1993).

The impact of reproductive health programmes on gender relations

The widespread availability of contraception has generally not been accompanied by a substantial shift towards gender equality in countries throughout the world; in most cases where women's economic and political power has increased, there is little or no evidence to suggest that access to contraception has been a significant factor (Schuler 1998). The weak link between contraceptive usage and gender equality can be attributed to two main factors. First, the introduction of a new technology alone cannot change power structures between women and men, which are embedded in society. Second, reproductive health programmes have seldom been designed and implemented in ways that empower women and promote gender equity; indeed, the accommodation of gender-based inequities has often reinforced patriarchal power structures. For example, the Bangladesh Family Planning Programme employs women in each community to deliver contraceptives to women in their homes on a national scale. This has resulted in high rates of contraceptive use and a drop in fertility rates. In failing to address issues of women's powerlessness such as their lack of mobility — instead bringing contraceptives to women's homes, and co-opting male decision-makers — the programme has reinforced ideologies which subordinate women (Schuler 1998).

It is critical to take gender inequalities in sexual decision-making into account when designing and providing reproductive health technologies. This approach, which is essential in the current crisis caused by HIV/AIDS, reflects the reproductive health

agenda of the UN Conference on Population and Development in Cairo, 1994 (ICPD 1994, McIntosh and Finckle 1995). In addition, there is growing awareness that gender inequality has serious implications for women's (and men's) health and well-being[4]. Gender relations are a key factor in women's and men's different levels of susceptibility and vulnerability to particular conditions and infections, including HIV; in their access to health-care and the variety of health services available to them; and in the social and health consequences of gender inequality (BRIDGE 1999). A pertinent example comes from Zambia, where a woman's explanation for her irregular, and therefore ineffective, use of the contraceptive pill was that her husband would take her packet of pills with him when he went on a trip, for fear of her being unfaithful (personal communication, 1999).

The present danger from the HIV/AIDS pandemic challenges health providers to meet gender-specific sexual health needs beyond reproduction (Cornwall, 1999). One response is to develop new technologies which will enable women to protect themselves from unwanted consequences of sex, using methods which do not depend on change in gender relations. For example, the female condom offers women another choice over which they have control; while female microbicides could, in the future, enable women to protect themselves from HIV without the knowledge of their partners and still conceive if desired. Another response is to confront, or strategically undermine, gender inequality through reproductive health programmes.

Technology, information strategies, and gender

Both 'hard' and 'soft' technologies can be used in information, education, and communication (IEC) strategies to promote reproductive health: the technologies are complementary and synergistic in raising awareness, changing behaviour, and helping people to use technologies successfully (Hubley 1993, Adler 1998). IEC approaches can be characterised by the degree of user participation in their planning, implementation, monitoring, and evaluation. We can think of a continuum from coercive methods including indoctrination at one end, through persuasion, advice, and education to user-centred activities, in which people identify and analyse their needs, and design activities to address them (Ewles and Simnett 1985, Adler et al. 1998). Historically, population programmes have tended to operate at the coercive end of the spectrum, in both face-to-face communication and mass media (Askew, 1988) The language used (of acceptors and drop-outs, targets and couple year protection, motivation, myths, and misconceptions) reflects an agenda set by the population movement rather than the community (Kenya National CBD Training Manual, 1991). With the broadening of the population agenda to sexual and reproductive health and rights following the UN conferences in Cairo in 1994, and Beijing in 1995, and with a growing interest in listening to and empowering the users, IEC approaches have become more participatory.

Programmes can use hard or soft technologies, or a combination of these, at any part of the continuum. While hard technologies can be used without face-to-face communication, as with posters and mass media including radio, they may also be used in combination with interpersonal communication: in radio-listening groups[5], through using video in the Stepping Stones programme[6], or by referring to printed materials when explaining how to use a contraceptive (Hubley 1993, Ewles and Simnett 1985). Community members can have a say by making their own videos to explain their needs to policy-makers, while health workers may hector or manipulate people to use contraceptive technologies in 'soft' face-to-face talks (Braden 1996).

A community-based distribution project in Zambia

In 1994, the Planned Parenthood Association of Zambia (PPAZ) initiated a community-based distribution (CBD) project in six districts in the Eastern Province, supported by the British Government's Department for International Development, with technical assistance from Options Consultancy Services. Using gender-sensitive participatory approaches to IEC, the programme aimed to increase the accessibility and acceptability of reproductive health services and to increase the practice of safer sex in rural communities, particularly among women and those living in poverty.

Zambia's Eastern province is predominantly rural, with poor roads, remote villages, and few channels of communication. The main occupation is subsistence farming, with many families experiencing seasonal food shortages. A situation analysis in Eastern Province revealed that 38 per cent of women live in female-headed households; almost half of these have no education. Forty per cent of teenage girls had begun childbearing, with 11 per cent of women married by the age of 14. The total fertility rate was 6.8, and the percentage of population using contraceptives (the contraceptive prevalence rate) 4.7 per cent. The incidence of sexually transmitted diseases (STDs) and HIV infection was high. Women outnumbered men, which pushed them into polygamous marriages or temporary unions, and encouraged them to have many children to keep these relationships. Communication on sexual matters was difficult: many men did not allow their wives to use contraception, and there were many concerns about the effects of modern methods of contraception on fertility and sexual relations. Many community groups saw AIDS as their main problem regarding reproductive health (Republic of Zambia 1994, Republic of Zambia/WHO 1995).

A feature — and major strength — of the CBD project is the close partnership between PPAZ and the state-run district health management teams and staff at Rural Health Centres (RHC). PPAZ and government staff trained 220 male and female CBD agents to counsel on the use of, and provide, condoms, oral contraceptives[7], and spermicides; to refer clients for injectibles, sterilisation, STD diagnosis and treatment; and to carry out IEC work.

In 1995, the first group of CBD agents (men and women in equal numbers) were selected by their communities in two districts and trained to provide services and use IEC methods to promote knowledge of reproductive health. The CBD agents were trained together with government staff, sharing their knowledge and perceptions of reproductive health in activities which drew on participants' personal experience. In 1996, some of these CBD agents were trained in participatory learning and action (PLA) methods[8] and the Stepping Stones approach. Based on this experience, in 1997 80 CBD agents from two new districts were trained using a revised one-month course.

After the initial training, the CBD agents were supervised and supported by RHC staff, by PPAZ, and by district supervisors at regular meetings and through refresher training and community visits. PPAZ is responsible for the overall development of the project, for the selection of agents, training, and logistics.

Participatory approaches used in the programme

The CBD project uses the following range of approaches to encourage the participation of both women and men:

- Non-directive counselling, rather than persuasion and direct advice;
- Interactive approaches, including songs, drama, and forum theatre[9] (Boal 1992, Bone et al. 1988), and the use of the flannelgraph[10] and picture cards to explore gender and relationship issues (Rohr-Rouendaal 1998, Linney 1995);
- Participatory learning and action (PLA) methods to identify needs, analyse causes and consequences, review experience of addressing problems, and find solutions for further action;
- Interactive drama techniques and exercises to develop communication and relationship skills, taken from the Stepping Stones programme[11];
- Participatory monitoring and evaluation.

The new agents began by mapping their catchment area, showing the available resources for reproductive health. They made seasonality calendars[12] to identify factors affecting reproductive health and opportunities for interventions (SHIP 1997, IPPF 1997). Factors which influenced gender relations included access to money for men and women, workloads, and climate. Conceptions and STD transmission peaked in the cold, dry season after harvest, when people had some leisure, enough cash to drink beer, and slept together for warmth. Daily and weekly routine diagrams showed how men and women spent their days, and enabled the agents to plan the best time to work with various peer groups.

The agents then facilitated single-sex groups of adolescent, young, and mature men and women. Each group drew pictures of joys and problems related to sexual and reproductive health. They used stones to rank and prioritise their problems, and flow-charts and role-play to analyse their causes and consequences. They also assessed the community's successes and failures in addressing the problem, and ranked the importance of different helpers and services, and their advantages and disadvantages. They finally tried to solve the priority problem, and agreed on an action plan. The CBD agents later helped them solve the other problems identified.

Role-play, games and discussion were used to explore the groups' expectations as women or men at their stage of life, and the positive and negative impact of these on their lives. For example, young women discussed the fact that they were expected to be sexually submissive to their husbands, even if they suspected their husbands to have an STD or HIV; while men felt that they were expected to seek sexual satisfaction outside marriage if their wives were unavailable for any reason.

Activities undertaken in the peer-groups focused on hopes and fears for the future; concepts of friendship, love, and marriage; personal risk-taking; and people's tendency to judge others. Participants practised communication skills through role-play (such as how to say what they would like sexually in an assertive way). The joint workshops provided an opportunity for men and women, young and old, to share common concerns and note differences, to build trust and co-operation, and to practise communicating about their lives. Often, this was the first opportunity for women and young people to voice their needs and concerns in public, and they found it empowering. As one adolescent girl said: 'I now feel confident to express myself in public. I have found my voice' (personal observation, 1997).

In the final stage of the process,each peer group could present to the whole community a 'special request' for a change in behaviour, often directed at another peer group,. In one village, adolescent girls asked older married men to stop pursuing them for sex. One year after the activity, this was reported to have resulted in a sustained reduction in this behaviour.

The CBD project's impact

In 1998, the project team, supervisors, CBD agents, and members of the Neighbour-hood Health Committees carried out an evaluation of the CBD project, using PLA techniques with peer groups, analysis of data collected routinely by CBD agents and government staff, and focus-group discussions with users of the CBD services, non-users, and those who had stopped using services. The range of techniques provided information on the positive and negative impacts of the project on the lives of community members and of the CBD agents themselves, and came up with suggestions for improving the programme. Reductions in the prevalence of STDs and malnutrition were reported by RHC staff, but statistics are not available at this time.

Number of clients using CBD services

On average, CBD agents reach between 150 and 200 new clients a year with contraceptive services. The contraceptive prevalence rate has more than doubled in areas where the project has been operating since 1996. CBD agents who were trained in 1996 have about 700 clients registered. On average, 40 per cent of clients use oral contraceptives, 7 per cent foam, and 53 per cent condoms. Male and female clients are equally represented, with on average 10 per cent under the age of 17 years. A quarter of male and 13 per cent of female clients are single.

Data on changes in health status and fertility rates are not available, but RHC staff report a drop in the number of cases of STD and malnutrition. The local courts that deal with cases of adultery, marital discord, divorce, and pregnancy outside marriage report a drop in the number of cases, which they attribute to the CBD project (internal documents, 1999).

Feedback on reproductive technologies

Both men and women in many of the peer groups reported that they appreciated modern contraceptives because they were easy to use, free and reliable. Between 40 to 60 per cent of women chose combined or low-dose oral contraceptives, and around 65 per cent continued to use them until they wished to conceive. Some women liked the combined contraceptive pill, because periods are very regular and there is less bleeding. Some users of the low-dose pill and contraceptive injections liked the absence of periods, because they did not have to worry about menstrual hygiene.

The most frequently mentioned negative effects of the contraceptive technologies were menstrual irregularities, infertility, and side effects associated with the pill and injectable hormonal methods. Fears about infertility stem from local understandings of reproductive anatomy and physiology, and misconceptions about how the pill works. Menstrual irregularities were a problem because sex during bleeding is taboo. Men complained about this side-effect, and reportedly sought other women. Some women who used injectable contraceptives and low-dose pills worried about what happened to the blood that is normally lost; some believed that it caused bloated stomachs and swollen legs.

The main problems reported with the condom as a contraceptive technology included breakage, which may increase as a result of a local preference for dry sex, very vigorous sex, or poor storage in hot conditions. Emergency contraception, for use when a condom breaks, is not yet openly available in this area of rural Zambia. It was reported that condoms are too big for some adolescents, whilst the rim can be tight and painful for the well-endowed. Condom disposal in communities with few latrines, and in cases of illicit sex, is not straightforward. Negative connotations of condom use were also a problem. Single people, adolescents, and those having extramarital sex were seen as the main users of condoms. It was considered insulting to suggest the use of a condom to a wife or committed girlfriend. However, the same meaning was not attached to the female condom, which was in high demand in the project. Married people appreciated it as a woman's method, with no side effects and offering protection against pregnancy and disease.

The impact of IEC techniques on gender relations and sexuality

Considering the impact of participatory IEC methods, women in particular appeared to feel empowered by the opportunity to speak out about their concerns at the joint work-shops. For instance, older women expressed their dislike of a traditional practice, whereby they were expected to show in specified sexual ways their gratitude for a gift of cloth, often purchased with money they had contributed to earning. The men seemed surprised that the women disliked the practice, and saw no reason to continue it. Adolescents spoke in public for the first time about their need for sex education and contraceptives. At the time, this appeared to be empowering, although the older men harassed the adolescent girls with provo-cative questions. However, it was later learned that this kind of exchange caused conflict and distress to some individuals, so the community agreed that the peer groups would share only what all members had agreed, and the CBD agents would act as mediators between the groups to discuss sensitive issues, using pictures or role play.

Work in single-sex peer groups gave people of different ages and sexes the chance to explore their needs and desires, and to gain confidence in speaking about sexual issues in a relatively safe space. They could rehearse together new ways of communicating and behaving sexually. They could take action to address their own gender needs, and the CBD agent could transmit their needs to others to bring about change. However, single-sex groups do not offer practice in talking to the opposite sex and in empathising with their concerns and feelings. Working with both men and women, and adolescents and older people, is essential for improving gender relations, and for achieving a better understanding of adolescents' needs by the community.

The PLA activity with peer groups gene-rated many potential CBD clients for counselling on contraceptive methods, STD transmission, and other sexual worries, and inspired other interventions aimed at improving gender relations and reproductive health in the peer groups. If the solutions were beyond the mandate of the CBD agents, they were encouraged to collaborate with other extension agents or sectors, such as the community development officer for income-generation.

Both men and women cited more harmonious marital relations as the most positive impact of the service-delivery component on sexual and gender relations. This was because couples were now using technologies which meant they could have sex at any time, even when their babies were small, without fear of starting another pregnancy. Women talked of regaining sexual desire after childbirth. The spacing of births achieved by contraceptive technologies meant that couples could enjoy sex without a baby lying beside them. One man commented, 'whether I turn to the left or right, all I smell is scented powder, not baby's urine as it used to be'. Community leaders reported that there were fewer marital quarrels, and women said that men stayed at home, together with their money, because they no longer felt the need for girlfriends. Women seemed to enjoy their sexuality more, and this was linked to a sense of empowerment: one talked about 'staying young and beautiful' and another of 'the freedom of working in the fields without a baby on my back'. During the evaluation, the service providers reported that male opposition to contraception has reduced since the CBD programme started, because the male CBD agents reach men and have time to counsel them properly.

Adolescents perceived the CBD project as positive. Girls reported that they could stay at school longer by avoiding teenage pregnancy. Some girls felt they could have affairs 'even with married men' without consequences. This is a good example of an intervention having positive impact for one group, while affecting another negatively:

such freedom might be empowering for young girls if they gain material benefits and pleasure, but not for the wives. Boys said that they were able to 'practise sex for future perfection without paying damages to pregnant girlfriends'. As a result of the CBD project, boys and girls were less likely to be forced into early marriages because of pregnancy and the need to legitimise sexual contact. Young people usually saw this as positive; however, some parents felt it was negative because they could not longer count on a dowry when their daughters married, and on the labour of sons-in-law.

Some findings indicated that in certain cases gender relations were worsened by the availability of contraceptives. This was cited half as frequently as the improvements in gender relations, and many disagreed, saying that it is not contraceptives which lead to promiscuity, but an individual's character. Some people thought that contraceptives were causing quarrels and divorce because of lack of trust and jealousy, especially in cases where contraceptives were used without the other partner knowing. The most frequently mentioned negative effect of greater use of contraceptive technologies was 'increased promiscuity' and, for these committed Christian communities, immorality. This was reported with reference to adolescents who were sexually active before marriage, and to adultery after marriage. A wife complained that condoms enabled her husband to chase 'anything in skirts', while some husbands worried that their wives could take lovers with impunity if they took the pill.

Some women found the constant sexual availability which some contraceptives allowed, even soon after childbirth, irksome or distressing. Previously, they had appreciated 'nights off' from demanding husbands during menstruation and at the fertile time (personal communication, CBD agents, Chipata). One man said that 'with a condom you can even have sex during the woman's menses'.

CBD agents encouraged clients as much as possible to talk to their partners about the decision to use contraceptives, and offered to counsel them individually or as a couple. However, where clients did exercise their right to confidentiality, this occasionally resulted in hostility and even violence from partners and parents, and in accusations of sexual relations during private counselling sessions between clients and CBD agents of the opposite sex. In principle, the CBD agents were expected to deal with clients of both sexes, unless the client felt uncomfortable with this.

The impact of involvement with the CBD project on the CBD agents themselves was also assessed. Many felt that their training has helped to improve gender relations with their marital partners. Women reported that they felt empowered to talk more confidently; and a male CBD agent reported that he and his colleagues had become 'less brutal and more caring'.

Future challenges for participatory approaches to gender and reproductive health

If reproductive health technologies are to fulfil their potential for improving sexual and reproductive health, it is essential to understand and address gender relations and sexuality. It is increasingly recognised that men and women of all ages need opportunities to share their ideas and feelings, explore their own attitudes, develop skills, and apply new knowledge to their own situations (Weiss 1998, IPPF 1997, Gordon 1992). Participatory approaches can transform gender relations and enable providers of reproductive health services to gain a better understanding of their clients' needs. Donors' growing interest in participation, partnerships, and the involvement of 'civil society' in development (ODA, 1995, IDS 1996, Hausman 1998) provides opportunities for transforming gender relations.

However, this focus also presents challenges which should not be underestimated.

Participatory approaches can help to unravel the complex links between reproductive and sexual health. Currently, new and distinct conceptualisations of sexuality and gender are arising, provoked by a realisation that, 'an important barrier in our efforts to understand gender relations is the difficulty in comprehending the links between sex and gender ' (Flax 1992, cited in Corrêa 1997). It may be that lessons learned from the application of participatory approaches can in turn help to establish clearer parameters for advancing the sexual and reproductive rights agenda.

Creative combinations of hard and soft technologies used as part of a participatory process can help to address gender relations and sexuality and enable people to use reproductive technologies in ways that enhance their lives. However, choices are limited by cost — both to the communities, and to the project. In the Zambian project, it was not feasible to use radio or video, since few people have access to these technologies. Even securing funds to purchase fuel for vehicles to distribute contraceptives to the project areas was a constant struggle. In this context, it was also seen as too costly to support a drama group to travel around the villages performing plays on sexual and reproductive health. Role-play, drama, and pictures created by project workers and the community themselves represented the most sustainable use of media.

This use of the 'soft' technology of participatory approaches to IEC is time-consuming for both project staff and community members, and demands considerable skills on the part of facilitators. Participatory approaches will only transform gender relations if the facilitators use them in such as way that people's values and attitudes are challenged. On some occasions, the use of interactive IEC activities reinforced negative gender stereotypes: one story used as a discussion-starter showed a woman having an affair with a travelling jewel dealer for money, and then infecting her husband with HIV. In the ensuing discussion, many people blamed the woman, saying that women are the source and transmitters of HIV. Stories created by agents reflect the attitudes of their creators, and it takes time to successfully challenge the gender biases of community workers.

It is not easy to predict the outcome of opening the floodgates in talking about sexuality. Issues of confidentiality and safety must be addressed from the start. However, it is impossible to guarantee confidentiality in a group, so people may put themselves at risk of gossip leading to harassment, conflict, or stigmatisation. If distressing issues are aired, this can lead to positive change if handled constructively; but it can also result in conflict, worsening the position of vulnerable people. It is important to establish support mechanisms for participants.

It is important to use participatory approaches in ways that benefit as many people as possible in the project area. There is a risk that intensive work with relatively small groups can result in feelings of exclusiveness and superiority among participants, who are often the better-off. This results in negative attitudes towards those who did not attend, and a lack of sharing. An evaluation of a project using the Stepping Stones approach in two rural communities in Uganda illustrated this finding (Actionaid et al. 1998).

Katie Chapman is Projects Manager and reproductive health programming specialist at Options Consultancy Services Limited (k.chapman@options.co.uk), which provides technical assistance to NGOs, donor agencies, and multilaterals on all aspects of reproductive, sexual, and maternal health programming. Options Consultancy Services Ltd., 129 Whitfield Street, London W1P 5RT, UK. Fax: +44 (0)171 388 1884.

Gill Gordon is a freelance consultant in sexual and reproductive health, and a Stepping Stones trainer. E-mail: gmgordon@netcomuk.co.uk

Notes

1 Gill Gordon has provided technical assistance to the programme discussed in this article through Options Consultancy Services since 1995.

2 Hard technologies include electronic, audio and print materials. Soft technologies include interpersonal communication activities such as counselling, small group work, interactive performing arts, and Participatory Learning and Action (Hubley 1993).

3 'Reproductive health is a state of complete physical, mental, and social well-being and not merely the absence of disease of infirmity, in all matters relating to the reproductive system and its functions and processes. The term therefore implies that people are able to have a satisfying and safe sex life and that they have the capability to reproduce and the freedom to decide if, when and how often to do so ... Sexual health aims to enhance life and personal relations and not merely counselling and care related to reproduction and sexually transmitted diseases.' (ICPD Programme of Action, Paragraph 7.3, United Nations 1994)

4 For a summary of how gender roles affect reproductive and sexual behaviour, see Population Reports Series J, No. 46 (October 1998).

5 In radio-listening groups, community members listen to an educational programme on the radio together and discuss it, using questions or activities suggested by the presenter or a local facilitator. The programme may also distribute print materials to listeners.

6 Stepping Stones is a practical approach to enabling women and men of all ages to explore their social, sexual, and psychological needs, to analyse the factors that

influence sexual interactions, and to make changes in their relationships. The approach includes a training package on communication and relationship skills for peer groups in communities, and on HIV/AIDS. It uses interactive drama, games, and video clips to encourage people to talk about their sexual lives and gender relations, and find ways to solve problems. The approach recognises that gender relations and gender inequity must be addressed in order to achieve the goal of better reproductive and sexual health (Welbourn 1995).

7 The CBD agents screen clients for oral contraceptives using a checklist, and ask clients to visit the Rural Health Centre (RHC) nurse for a blood pressure and health check before collecting their next three cycles of pills.

8 Robert Chambers defines PLA as a growing family of approaches and methods that enable community groups to share and enhance their knowledge of local conditions, to analyse, to plan, and to act (Chambers 1997).

9 In forum theatre, actors perform a short drama to demonstrate a problematic situation. The audience is invited to think how a particular character could behave differently to improve the situation, and any member of the audience can intervene to change the action, taking on the role of one of the characters. The group then discusses whether the new behaviour would work, and others try their ideas. The drama then continues.

10 A flannelgraph is a board covered with flannel or a rough material such as a blanket, and a set of pictures printed on flannel or drawn on cardboard that will stick to the board. The pictures are used to tell a story or show a sequence of events. They are put up one by one as the story is told, with audience participation, or the group uses the pictures to tell their own stories.

11 As an outcome of the first training course, the Stepping Stones manual was adapted for use in the CBD project in Zambia by Gill Gordon (Gordon 1997).

12 A seasonality calendar is a diagram that shows changes in health, climate, food supplies, income, sexual activity, workloads, and anything relevant to the topic at hand, over a one-year period.

References

Actionaid, Bedd Barna, KAHCAE, AEGY (1998) *'The teeth that are close together can bite the meat': A participatory review of Stepping Stones in two communities in Uganda*, Actionaid, London.

Adler, M, et al. (1998) *Sexual Health and Health Care: Sexually Transmitted Infections. Guidelines for Prevention and Treatment*, DFID Health and Population Occasional Paper, pp.43-53.

Askew, I (1988) *A comparative analysis of community participation projects in South Asia with policy and programme recommendations for family planning associations*, IPPF Occasional Series, Community Participation.

Bledsoe, C, Banja, F and Hill, A (1998) 'Reproductive Mishaps and Western Contraception: An African Challenge to Fertility Theory', in *Population and Development Review* Vol. 24, No.1.

Boal, A (1992) *Games for Actors and non-Actors*, Routledge, London.

Braden, S (1996) 'Video work with communities', *Anthropology in Action*, Vol. 3, No. 1.

BRIDGE (1999) *Development and Gender in Brief, Issue 7: Health and well-being*, Institute of Development Studies, University of Sussex, Brighton.

Chambers, R (1997) *Whose Reality Counts?*, Intermediate Technology Publications.

Cornwall, A (1999) 'Beyond Reproduction: changing perspectives on gender and health', in BRIDGE (1999) *Development and Gender in Brief, Issue 7*.

44

Corrêa, S (1997) 'From Reproductive Health to Sexual Rights: Achievements and Future Challenges', in *Reproductive Health Matters*, No. 10.

Dixon-Mueller, R (1993i) *Population Policy and Women's Rights: Transforming Reproductive Choice*, Praeger, Westport, Connecticut/ London.

Dixon-Mueller, R (1993ii) 'The Sexuality Connection in Reproductive Health', in *Studies in Family Planning*, Vol. 24, No. 5.

Ewles, L and Simnett, I (1985) *Promoting health: A practical guide to health education*, John Wiley & Sons Ltd.

Gordon, G and Kanstrup, C (1992) 'Sexuality — the Missing Link in Women's Health', in *IDS Bulletin*, Vol 23, No. 1.

Hardon, A (1994) 'The development of contraceptive technologies: a feminist critique', in *Gender and Development*, Vol. 2, No. 2, Oxfam GB, Oxford.

Hardon, A (1997) 'Contesting claims on the safety and acceptability of anti-fertility vaccines', in *Reproductive Health Matters*, No. 10.

Hartmann, B (1987) *Reproductive Rights and Wrongs: The global politics of population control and contraceptive choice*, Harper and Row, New York.

Hubley, J (1993) *Communicating Health*, MacMillan/TALC.

International Conference on Population and Development (1994) *Programme for Action*.

IDS (1996) *The power of participation*, IDS Policy Briefing, Issue 7.

IPPF (1997) *Sexual and Reproductive Health: A new approach with communities*, Banson Press.

The Johns Hopkins School of Public Health (1994) *Opportunities for Women Through Reproductive Choice*, Population Reports Series M, No. 12, Baltimore.

The Johns Hopkins School of Public Health (1998) *New Perspectives on Men's Participation*, Population Reports Series J, No. 46, Baltimore.

Kenya National Council for Population and Development (1991) National training manual for CBD programmes.

Linney, B (1995) *People, Pictures and Power: Health Images*, Macmillan, London.

McIntosh, CA and Finckle, JL (1995) 'The Cairo Conference on Population and Development: A New Paradigm?', in *Population and Development Review*, Vol.21, No 2.

ODA (1995) 'Note on enhancing stakeholder participation in aid activities', internal paper, London.

Republic of Zambia/WHO (1995) Zambia Contraceptive Needs Assessment.

Republic of Zambia/ODA (1994) 'Project Memorandum on Family Planning Services Component', report.

Rohr-Rouendaal, P (1997) *Where There Is No Artist*, IT Publications, London.

Schuler, SR (1998) *In Accommodating, Reinforcing Gender Inequity in Family Planning Programs*, JSI Working Paper No. 14, JSI Research and Training Institute, Inc., Boston.

SHIP (Sexual Health Information Pack) (1997) Institute of Development Studies, University of Sussex.

Sen G, Germain, A, Chen, L (eds.) (1994) *Setting A New Agenda: Sexual and reproductive health rights*, Harvard University Press, Boston, Massachusetts.

Welbourn, A (1995) *Stepping Stones: Strategies for Hope*, Training material No. 1, TALC.

Weiss, E (1998) 'Final report of the Women and AIDS research program', International Centre for Research on Women, New York.

Rural development and women: What are the best approaches to communicating information?

Joyce A Otsyina and Diana Rosenberg

The availability of improved agricultural and environmental conservation technologies might suggest that we can relatively easily improve the living conditions of rural farmers. However, the experience of a project in Tanzania shows that men's and women's use of technologies are intricately linked with social and cultural factors such as the gender division of labour.

There is no lack of technologies and scientific discoveries which could bring about economic growth and rural development in poor countries. The main problem is the lack of effective communication strategies and methods (Singh 1981). Studies over the past three decades have revealed that in many parts of Africa, most development programmes meet with little success because ineffective communication strategies are used (Mchombu 1992, FAO 1990).

If the aim of rural development is to alleviate poverty, then development information must be communicated in a way that will not prevent or deter women from actively participating in development activities. The poorest and the most needy in most rural societies are women. They carry heavy responsibilities for farming, for feeding their families, and often take the role of head of the household (Spore 1993). Timetables for development activities often take no account of the time women spend on household chores. Other reasons for women's marginalisation from communications and information on development

activities can be based on culture or religion. In some parts of the world, cultural and religious barriers prevent male extension officers from having close contact with women. This is particularly true in Muslim countries, where male extension officers may be forbidden to speak to women (Rosenberg 1986). Husbands, too, can sometimes be reluctant to allow their wives to learn new ideas from men who are not part of their communities (ibid.).

With the identification of communication strategies as a stumbling block in rural development comes the need to find out what means and methods of communication work best and in what circumstances. In 1992, such a study was carried out in Tanzania (Otsyina 1993). It examined the strategies employed by an extension agency in communicating development information to farmers. Within the general objective of determining the effectiveness of the methods used to mobilise all farmers to participate fully in the development process, our research also aimed to discover how well the needs of women were being met.

Shinyanga and the Hifadhi Ardhi Shinyanga project

The Shinyanga region is situated in north-west Tanzania, south of Lake Victoria. It has a total area of 50,764 square kilometres, more than half of which is arable land, 12,079 is grazing land, and 7,544 forest reserves. Annual rainfall ranges from 600 to 1,200mm across the region, but during the dry season, from May to November, total rainfall is under 50mm (Darkoh 1982). The region has a population of 1,674,000, about 95 per cent of whom live in rural areas. In contrast to a national male literacy rate of 79.4 and a female rate of 56.8 (UN 1998), in Shinyanga the literacy rate at the time of the research was estimated at below 25 per cent, with women making up the majority of the illiterate group (Bureau of Statistics 1988). The inhabitants of the region are mostly Sukuma, who are predominantly agro-pastoralists. Kiswahili and Kisukuma are the most widely spoken languages.

The Shinyanga region is one the most degraded and deforested areas in Tanzania, because vast areas were cleared to eradicate tsetse flies and quela birds during the 1920s and 1930s (Glasgow 1960). In addition, the unsuccessful *Ujamaa* (villagisation) programme under the then President Nyerere, and the introduction and expansion of cash cropping, particularly cotton, in the 1950s and 1960s further contributed to land degradation. This caused low and decreasing soil fertility, scarcity of water and fuelwood, and a decline in grazing areas (NORAD 1988).

Soil conservation measures were introduced into Sukumaland by the colonial authorities as early as 1920 (Berry and Townshend 1973), but their measures failed because implementation depended on a system of coercion and punishment (Fuggles-Couchman 1964). After Independence, interest in conservation was revived and several projects were started, with more success. These included the Hifadhi Ardhi Dodoma (HADO) project and, in 1986, the Hifadhi Ardhi Shinyanga (HASHI) project.

The HASHI project is a soil conservation and afforestation programme. It was established in 1986 under the Ministry of Lands, Natural Resources and Tourism, in the division of Forestry and Bee Keeping, and is funded by the Norwegian Agency for Development (NORAD). HASHI's main task is to undertake, within the bounds of the resources and capabilities available, desertification-control practices which are ecologically sustainable, financially attractive, and culturally acceptable. They are also intended to help create a diversified economy, in order to raise the standard of living of the rural poor of in Shinyanga Region, most of whom are women. Thus HASHI's aim is not to change the existing gender relations between men and women, but to help them improve their standards of living.

In order to achieve this, HASHI tries to raise farmers' awareness and provides extension services in tree-planting and soil conservation. It differs from many rural development projects in aiming to promote people's participation in decision-making and in solving their own problems. HASHI operates with the guiding principle: 'Go to the people. Live among them. Start with what they know. Build on what they have.'

But, even after so many years of HASHI's involvement and interaction with the rural communities, there is no clear indication that women are actively participating in the programmes or adopting the ideas and practices being communicated (Shao et al. 1992). Hence there was a need to assess the communication strategies being used.

The research

Two of the six districts in Shinyanga — Shinyanga Rural and Meatu — were selected for this assessment. Five villages in each district (most of which have HASHI projects) were involved. The research was survey-based, using semi-structured interviews, supplemented by the use of less formal techniques such as observation, group discussions at village-level, and informal discussions with knowledgeable individuals. A stratified sampling approach was adopted, using gender as the basis for identifying and comparing problems specific to men and women. Two hundred farmers were interviewed; an additional 400 were contacted through group discussions. The farmers interviewed were selected at random from 200 households, 20 from each village (ten men and ten women). No particular attention was focused on female-headed households in this study. Where they happened to be in the sample, they were interviewed. Otherwise, women were interviewed as women, regardless of their status within their household.

The raw data obtained from responses to the interview schedules was coded and subjected to computer analysis. The qualitative data obtained was summarised, and used to support the data from individual questionnaires.

Personal characteristics of women and men in the area

Any method of communicating information must choose a strategy which appeals to and can be understood by the target group. Before assessing the strategies used by

HASHI, it is therefore necessary to examine the personal characteristics of the inhabitants of Sukumaland and any differences between men and women.

Education

Data on the educational background of respondents is presented in Table 1. Forty per cent had no formal education, while 43 per cent had primary education, and only a few had post-primary education (secondary school or teacher-training college). However, 14.5 per cent had managed to go through adult education literacy programmes. In general, women had lower education levels than men, with 46 per cent as opposed to 34 per cent having no education at all, and fewer obtaining primary or other education at every level. The Sukuma traditionally do not consider it important to educate women, because they are a source of wealth and labour. Therefore, women are married off early by their parents (ibid.).

Gender differences in farming and herding

Whereas almost all respondents (96 per cent), whether men or women, were engaged mainly in crop farming, and in herding as a secondary activity, there were major differences in ownership of land and type of animal herded.

In the case of male respondents, land holdings range from 0.5 to 250 hectares, with an average of 12 hectares. Only 8 per

Table 1: Education background of respondents

Level	% of respondents		
	Male	**Female**	**Total sample**
No education	34	46	40
Adult education	16	13	14.5
Primary education	46	40	43
Secondary education	1	0	0.5
Teacher Training college	2	1	1.5
Bible school	1	0	0.5

NB: *Respondents were allowed more than one response. Thus percentages do not add up to 100. This applies to subsequent tables in the text.*

Problem	% of respondents
Distance to source	78.1
Must hire trailer for transport	31.3
Scarcity of firewood	30.2
Must get permission	20.8
Difficult to harvest	9.4
High prices	2.1
Must hire labour to cut	2.1

Table 2: Problems relating to firewood encountered by women

cent of respondents possess the maximum land holding: most men owned between 0.5 and 8 hectares. In contrast, some 70 per cent of female respondents had no land holdings of their own; they depended entirely on their husbands and relatives. Even those with land of their own possessed only between 0.5 and 5 hectares. This land was acquired through inheritance, either from late husbands or from relatives. Land, according to Sukuma culture, is owned by men; women depend entirely on their husbands. A woman cannot own land unless it is specifically given to her by her parents, husband, or her husband's relatives. However, an unmarried woman can have a plot allocated to her by the village government or hire one for a period of 2 years (Shao et al. 1992). Women in general cannot therefore make any decision that involves the development of the land. This affects the extent to which they can employ conservation and afforestation technologies, such as planting trees for fuelwood and other products.

Seventy per cent of all households interviewed during our research kept livestock: cattle, goats, sheep, and chickens. Cattle is the most common livestock, owned mainly by men. Cows are multifunctional and serve as a source of accumulating wealth and savings. They are an important economic and social asset in Sukuma society. Eighty-six per cent of

respondents who owned cattle were men, and only 16 per cent of female respondents claimed absolute ownership of cattle. Almost a quarter of women did own a proportion of a household's cattle for milk production (usually between one and five cows). Chickens are associated with women, while goats and draft animals are associated with men. In Sukuma culture, cattle belong to men and wives have no part in decision-making over cattle. At the same time, a woman can own cattle if she is not married, if she inherits them from her husband, or if she has been given them by a relative. In this case, she makes decisions concerning them (Shao et al. 1992)

The problem of fuelwood

Obtaining fuelwood is a woman's duty, and 96 per cent of female respondents said they had problems finding sufficient firewood throughout the year. The few women (4 per cent) who did not identify this as a major problem had husbands with large land holdings and large uncultivated woodlots. Because of the difficulties involved in fuelwood collection, women are forced to use cow dung, maize cobs, and cotton twigs as sources of fuel.

The firewood problems encountered by women are presented in Table 2. A major problem is scarcity, and women often walked long distances — between 1 and 30km, but 9.5km on average — to collect firewood. During the rainy season, flooding makes most places inaccessible. During these times, women are also occupied with farming activities. The dry season brings with it less farm work, so women usually collect firewood in the dry season and store it for the rainy season. However, 33 per cent of female respondents said that they had to buy in additional firewood before the end of the rainy season. An ox-cart load (about 8-9m^3) was reported to last an average family for at least three months.

Firewood lasts much longer if improved stoves are used: in the research, women testified that the amount of firewood used in one week would last for two weeks in improved stoves, making a significant saving. Improved stoves are based on the three-stone stoves usually used by women in the rural areas. In the improved design, clay is built around the stones leaving just enough space for firewood, cooking pot and smoke, which saves fuel. All that is needed in their construction is clay and three stones, which are easily found in the locality. Women are aware of all the good aspects of these stoves, as was revealed during group discussions. One woman commented: 'We know from the few women who have the improved stoves that they use less firewood; their cooking pots do not get as dark as those of us using stones, and also they do not have smoke getting into their eyes. We all envy women who have these stoves.'

Effectiveness of communication strategies

HASHI has used various means of communication in order to raise awareness of conservation issues, and to train people in the techniques of soil conservation and afforestation. The means used include village meetings, film shows, radio, seminars, study tours, and demonstration plots.

Awareness

Table 3 indicates which channels of communication were most effective in creating awareness. There are considerable differences between men and women.

Village meetings were the most popular channel of communication with both sexes, but men appeared to have benefited more (71 per cent) than women (57.7 per cent) from information shared in this manner. This is because village meetings, although compulsory for all, are usually held in the morning, when women are most occupied with household chores such as going to weed or searching for water. Women are also given less opportunity to discuss issues because, in Sukuma culture, their views are not very much respected (Shao et al. 1992). Although the percentage of women who attend these meetings was quite encouraging (more than half), they did not seem to the researchers to be participating fully in the discussion, and

Table 3: *Significance of different channels in communicating information for awareness*

Channel	% of respondents	
	Male	**Female**
Village meeting	71.0	57.7
Film show	66.0	55.7
Radio	29.0	14.4
School	5.0	10.3
Seminar	7.0	5.2
Neighbours	1.0	8.2
Posters	6.0	0
School children	2.0	4.1

Form of training	% of respondents	
	Male	Female
HASHI demonstration plots	70.0	50.0
School demonstration plots	10.0	21.9
UWT demonstration plots	4.0	15.6
Village meeting	12.0	6.3
Seminar	4.0	3.1
Study tour	2.0	6.3
Village community wood lot	4.0	3.1
Youth camp	8.0	0
Farm visit	4.0	3.1

Table 4: Main forms of training

this would clearly influence the degree and nature of their participation in HASHI's development activities. Village meetings did not seem, therefore, to be an effective means of communicating ideas to women.

Film shows and radio broadcasts were also popular among both sexes, but more so among men. One major drawback to film shows is that they often take place at night, when women are either reluctant to go out in the dark or must stay home to take care of the children. Due to the scattered nature of settlements in this part of the country, women who live in areas further away from the centre of activities were particularly unlikely to attend.

In contrast to men, women depend far more on secondary sources for information, such as neighbours and school children who have attended the meetings and film shows. Informal communications networks are very important to them. In addition, they rely what they learned in primary school. One woman said: 'You know, we are women. We learn a lot from gossip, and from our neighbours on our way to the farm or the riverside. We also learn a lot from our children in the evenings. They tell us a lot about the things they are learning at school, and this information helps us'.

Training

During HASHI's training sessions, farmers were taught various ways of soil conservation and afforestation (mainly how to plant trees), and women were taught how to make and use improved stoves. Women and men were trained together.

Table 4 presents the main forms of training in which male and female respondents participated. Half of all male respondents had training, compared to only one-third of women. The predominant form was the use of HASHI's demonstration plots. The number of people involved in this type of training is high, because the community controls it. Village leaders make training on HASHI demonstration plots compulsory for every adult, and are also involved in organising them. Seventy per cent of the men, compared to 50 per cent of the women, were trained on HASHI plots. Seminars and study tours, on the other hand, were just for a chosen few (village leaders and progressive farmers) and are organised by HASHI staff. Only a few trainees were chosen due to financial constraints.

HASHI also used Umoja wa Wanawake wa Tanzania (UWT), the official government-sponsored women's organisation, as a means of training women in cultivating woodlots to provide fuel. On the face of it, this should have been successful, since such training would meet women's specific needs. However, women's reactions to this idea expressed during group discussions, although not overt, indicated that some of the women were suspicious of UWT. It is not perceived as 'traditional', but as a group imposed from outside. They were therefore not enthusiastic about becoming members. In fact, only 15.6 per cent of female respondents were reached through UWT, and its effectiveness as a channel for communicating with rural women is therefore questionable.

The main method of communication used by HASHI for training on making and using improved stoves was to choose women, usually members of traditional women's groups, from the various districts and bring them together for a seminar, usually in Shinyanga town, Afterwards, the women were supposed to return to their villages and teach other women the skills of improved stove making.

From communication to practice

The ideas and techniques that were put into practice reflect on the effectiveness of the communication strategies. These are presented in Table 5. For both men and women, tree planting at the homestead was the predominant activity adopted, probably because it is the most practical and the one most emphasised by HASHI.

The slightly higher percentage of women is probably accounted for by the fact that, in addition to the seedlings supplied directly by HASHI to the farmers, some were brought home by school children and given to their mothers who did the planting. A higher percentage of women also planted trees on the farms; but then women spend more time working on the farms than men and might have been ordered by their husbands to plant the seedlings. The really surprising result is that only 5 per cent of female respondents made and used improved stoves, particularly as special seminars involving only women were organised. This finding is discussed in the next section.

Both male and female farmers showed enthusiasm for some of the new ideas and would like to put them into practice in due course. Man liked the idea of private woodlots — 40 per cent of those interviewed said they would like to establish one — and women that of improved stoves (50 per cent) and woodlots (25 per cent). Lack of land, seedlings, skills, and equipment were cited as reasons for

Table 5: Main ideas put into practice

Ideas	% of respondents	
	Male	Female
Tree planting at homestead	65.5	69.7
Leaving trees on farm (not felling)	17.2	3.9
Planting trees at UWT farm	0	6.6
Setting up tree nursery	4.6	1.3
In situ conservation	4.6	0
Planting fruit trees	3.4	2.6
Making contour ridges	3.4	2.6
Planting trees on farms	3.4	11.8
Making improved stoves	0	5.3

the delay in putting things learned into practice. Respondents also mentioned the problem of lack of water and the destructive activities of termites. These reasons did not differ between men and women, although women more frequently cited lack of skills.

The adoption of improved stoves

Only a few women owned land or cattle, and thus they could not participate as actively as men in conservation activities such as tree planting on farms or fodder developments. It seemed that the technologies likely to be more readily adopted by women were those which improved their standard of living, but did not involve the use of land or benefit livestock. The adoption of improved stoves by women is an activity which, in theory, can significantly reduce a woman's workload, which a woman has control over without any interference from men, and which will also help women contribute indirectly to the conservation of the environment (Everts 1998). Moreover, spending less time or money on finding firewood would improve standards of living.

As stated above, the rate of adoption of the improved stoves in Shinyanga was low. Only 5 per cent of the women sampled actually adopted the use of improved stoves. But most of them (50 per cent) were aware of their value and wanted to have them. However, lack of technical skills meant that their adoption was delayed. One woman told us: 'We are very much aware of the benefits of improved stoves and we are all very anxious to have them in our homes. But you know what? We do not have the skills for making them; only few women were trained to come back and teach us. They failed to teach us because they are just not the right people who can teach us. They were not chosen by us so we can't feel free to approach them.'

Although most female respondents were aware that people within the locality had been trained to teach them about the new stoves, there appear to have been no special efforts to learn the skills. One of the women who had been trained said that she had attempted to run classes, but that none of the women in the village had attended.

In our view, the most likely cause for this failure lies in the way technical information in which is communicated to rural women. Traditional women's groups, from which the trainees were chosen, are strong and form a major traditional system of information sharing. Since the groups originated from within the community and were shaped and controlled by it, their use by HASHI should have been a most effective way of spreading ideas. What went wrong was that HASHI staff themselves chose the trainees, without consulting the other women in the groups. This made them suspicious, and they were therefore reluctant to learn the new skills. What might have been an effective channel of communication was therefore crippled from the outset. Secondly, there was a problem in the number of women trained. Seminars are expensive to conduct, as participants have to be taken care of financially. Therefore only a few were trained and it was not possible for them to make a major impact. If the women themselves have been given the opportunity to select those they would learn from and if the training had been done in the locality in the form of village workshops, then more results would have been achieved.

The present situation: An update

In 1998, UNDP conducted a Participatory Poverty Assessment in Shinyanga to help in the eradication of poverty in the region. Even though the study was specifically on women and their information needs, it is interesting to note that just as in the earlier study of 1992, the information gap between women and men is still evident. Most women seem not to be aware of their rights in society — as wives, mothers, and, more generally, as citizens who are equal to their male counterparts. For example, most women are not aware of the fact that they can seek redress in court if molested by their husbands, or can fight for the right to inheritance at the death of their husbands. The 'top-down' approach to information communication by field workers is still in use. The same communication methods are used for both men and women without considering the role of women in society, and men continue to be suspicious of the acquisition and skills by their womenfolk (Otsyina 1998).

Some conclusions

In Shinyanga, women continue to be the poorest group in the community, since they have little land at their disposal and few cattle. They therefore stand to benefit most from new ideas in soil conservation and afforestation. However, our 1992 study revealed that in fact male farmers benefited most. The technologies introduced tended to be concerned with activities which are traditionally done by men, while no attempt was made to challenge this gender division of labour. Future research will focus on female-headed households and the impact of HASHI's activities on them. To date, HASHI's aim has been to help everyone, especially women, to improve upon their living conditions, but it has wished to do this without interfering with the culture of the people.

HASHI also failed to use communication channels that takes into account existing socio-economic differences between the genders. The same sorts of communication strategies were used for men and women. The most used channels of communication — village meetings and film shows — were more accessible to men than to women. This is partly due to cultural constraints, and partly to the fact that women are occupied with household chores at the time when such activities take place. Other forms of training — such as seminars — were dominated by a minority of privileged men. A typical comment on this was: 'We can see what our neighbours are doing. The things being practised are nice. We however do not understand what they are practising. They were just selected by HASHI staff, with the help of some village leaders. To us, they are favourites and the privileged in our society. We, the poor ones, have been left out. How can we follow their footsteps if we do not know what they are doing?'.

The introduction of improved stoves was specifically aimed at women, with the object of helping women solve their fire-wood problems and improve their living conditions, but it failed because of ineffective communication strategies. Women rely far more than men do on informal information networks. Their participation in the development process and their enthusiasm for the adoption of ideas could be improved if information was communicated to them on a household basis, in addition to group work. Attention also needs to be paid to the natural suspicions of men in a traditional society towards the acquisition of knowledge and skills by their womenfolk. Men must be made aware of everything that is being introduced to women; there must be more integration of communication methods. At the same time, more use of female extension workers could overcome cultural constraints.

In addition to the strategy of approaching women within their households, women's isolation needs to be overcome. Because of the nature of their household and farming duties, women tend to be tied far more to the area of their homes. More training in their localities through village workshops would encourage the active participation of women. Previous studies (Rosenberg 1986) have revealed that communication is more effective if done through events that bring women together. Workshops for women at village level would enable information to be shared with, and between, as many women as possible.

The debate on this important issue still continues. How best can women be reached? What are the most appropriate methods to be used, taking into consideration cultural and environmental conditions, and what are the contributions of field workers as individuals to the information problem of women? All these issues have to be thoroughly investigated, to help find lasting solutions to women's information problems.

Joyce Otsyina is from Ghana. She worked at the University of Ghana and has recently completed her M.Phil. in Library Studies at the University Ghana. She now lives in Tanzania, c/o ICRAF, PO Box 797, Shinyanga, Tanzania.

Diana Rosenberg is Head of Special Programmes, International African Institute, SOAS, Thornhaugh Street, Russell Square, London WC1 0XG, UK.

References

Aboyade, BA (1984) 'Making the library relevant in a non-literate society: The future of library and information services in Nigeria', Nigerian Libraries, Vol. 20.

Barrow et al. (1988) 'Soil conservation and afforestation in Shinyanga region: Potentials and constraints', mission report to NORAD.

Berry, L and Townshend, J (1973) 'Soil conservation policies in the arid and semi-arid regions of Tanzania: A historical perspective', in Rapp, A, Berry, L, and Temple, PH (eds.) *Studies in soil erosion in Tanzania*, BRALUP Research Monograph 1, University of Dar es Salaam.

Brandstorm, P (1985) 'The agro-pastoral dilemma: Under utilization or over exploitation of land among the Sukuma of Tanzania', Working Papers in African Studies 8, Department of Cultural Anthropology, Uppsala.

Darkoh, MBK (1987) 'Combating desertification in the arid and semi-arid lands of Tanzania', in *Journal of Arid Environments*, Vol. 12.

Everts, S (1998) *Gender and Technology: Empowering women, engendering development*, Zed Books, London.

FAO (1990) 'Communication Strategies for Rural Development: a Case Study of the Use of Campaigns in Lesotho', a development communication case study, FAO, Rome.

Fortmann, L and Rocheleau (1985) 'Women and agroforestry: Four myths and three case studies', in *Agroforestry Systems*, Vol. 2.

Fuggles-Couchman, N (1964) *Agricultural change in Tanganyika (1945-60)*, Food Research Institute, Stanford University.

Glasgow, JP (1960) 'Shinyanga: A review of the work of the Tsetse Research Laboratory', in *East African Agricultural and Forestry Journal*, July.

Mchombu, KJ (1992) 'Rural development information communication in Africa: Creating conditions for success', in *Information Trends*, Vol.5, No.2.

Mchombu, KJ (1986) 'Communication of information to "barefoot extension agents"', in Proceedings of the Seventh Meeting of the Standing Conference of Eastern, Central and Southern African Libraries, Botswana Library Association, Gaborone.

Menon, V (1966) 'What hope for the future of development communication?', in *Media in Development*, Vol. 33.

Otsyina, JA (1998) 'Communication of development information to rural communities: A case study of information communication in HASHI's soil conservation and afforestation project, Shinyanga, Tanzania', M.Phil. dissertation, Department of Library and Archival Studies, University of Ghana.

Rosenberg ,DB (1986) 'Repackaging in scientific and technical information for illiterate and semi-literate users: a case study of the Southern Sudan', in Proceedings of the Seventh Meeting of the Standing Conference of Eastern, Central and Southern African Libraries, Botswana Library Association, Gaborone, pp.8-22.

Shao, IF, Mboma, LMR, Semakafu, AM (1992) 'Traditional management of natural resources with emphasis on women: The case study of Shinyanga rural district', report submitted to NORAD, Institute of Development Studies, Dar es Salaam.

Singh, KN (1981) 'The need for a communication strategy for rural development', in Crouch, BR and Chamala, S (eds.) *Extension education and rural development, Vol.2: Experience in strategies for planned change*, Wiley, Chichester.

Spore (1993) 'Woman's rightful place?', *Bulletin of the Centre for Agricultural and Rural Co-operation*, Vol. 44, p.3.

Tanzania (1988) The population census: preliminary report, Bureau of Statistics, Ministry of Finance, Economic Affairs and Planning, Dar es Salaam.

Williams, PJ (1985) 'Women and forestry', special paper presented at the XI World Forestry Congress, Mexico City.

UN (1998) *Human Development Report*, UN, Washington DC.

Skilled craftswomen or cheap labour? Craft-based NGO projects as an alternative to female urban migration in northern Thailand

Rachel Humphreys

Rather than challenging stereotypical perceptions of certain abilities as 'women's skills', NGOs in northern Thailand working with craft producers tend to perpetuate the low values accorded these skills, both in cultural and economic terms.

In the predominantly agricultural villages of north and north-east Thailand, exquisite silk and cotton textiles are still hand-woven and decorated by women, who learn the skills from their mothers. Proficiency in these skills conveys status on a young woman in the village, because traditional beliefs hold that a good weaver possesses womanly virtues and will make a good wife. This article uses the example of ThaiCraft, a Thai NGO and alternative trade organisation (ATO), to discuss development projects specifically set up in order to provide an alternative to female urban migration, through the employment of young women in income-generating home-based craft projects. ThaiCraft focuses on promoting and supporting the traditional technologies of textile production, and is one of the larger of the many NGOs working in this field.

The north, particularly the north-east, are among the poorest regions in Thailand, and economic hardship allied to a lack of opportunities for paid work makes urban migration necessary for many. For young village women, there are two main avenues of work in urban areas: factory work and prostitution. To prefer to send daughters to work in urban areas is a rational strategy for families: a study of households in north-east Thailand found that on average 28 per cent of household income was remitted by absent daughters (Archavanitkul and Guest in Skrobanek et al. 1997), and in general daughters remit far more than sons (Sainsbury 1997). Other young women may be forced out of craft work and into the urban employment market at some point, since the markets for traditional handmade products — the tourist market, the expatriate market within Thailand, and the overseas market — are both limited and unreliable. This is particularly true of the overseas market, which can evaporate in the case of a recession (Harris 1997).

Home-based craft projects tend to be seen by their supporters as protective and redemptive; they perpetuate ideas of women hand-weavers as virtuous and industrious, and a perception of the complex skills required in traditional weaving as being 'natural' to women. This contributes to these skills being seen as 'non-skills' outside the village, and specifically in the factories where these skills are in demand. Research has shown that perceptions of women as unskilled labour are linked to low wages and poor working conditions, and that projects such as those run by ThaiCraft could evolve strategies to improve young women's longer-term chances of securing better paid, more fulfilling, secure work.

Much of the research for this article was carried out in 1994 when I was working in Thailand, and visited some of the weaving villages of the north and north-east. I also draw on project literature and publicity material from ThaiCraft.

Craft and textile-based NGO projects in Thailand

Craft or textile-based development projects are becoming increasingly popular with NGOs, local people, donors and local, national and international authorities; a prominent motivation for supporting them is that they can offer sustainable livelihoods to local people while attempting to preserve Thailand's rich cultural heritage and artisan communities (ThaiCraft 1997, 4).

ThaiCraft was set up in 1992 and is based in Bangkok. At its inception, ThaiCraft was initially run largely by volunteers, most of whom were expatriate Japanese, British, and American women; most of them were in Bangkok as accompanying partners of male breadwinners. ThaiCraft's publicity material and information, which was originally produced only in English and Japanese, explicitly reveals that the expatriate market is also the primary target market of the organisation. Recently, information has also been produced in Thai, and there has been a drive to recruit more Thai volunteers and paid staff at all levels of the organisation. However, the expatriate volunteer base continues to be extremely important, both in terms of the day-to-day running of the organisation, and the success of its sales in Bangkok (ThaiCraft 1994, ThaiCraft 1997, ThaiCraft March 1998).

ThaiCraft works with over 60 community-based artisan groups throughout Thailand, including members of Thailand's Hill Tribe minority groups and refugee groups. Most of ThaiCraft's producers are women. The organisation states that its aims are to help craftspeople achieve a fair income for their work and to preserve the beauty and skill of Thai craft traditions (ThaiCraft News, April 1998). ThaiCraft aims to achieve this by 'building dynamic educational partnerships among producers, volunteers, and the public' (ThaiCraft 1997, 4) and by disseminating information about producers' cultures and traditional crafts, while employing appropriate marketing techniques (ThaiCraft Manager's Viewpoint 1995). A significant proportion of Thai-Craft's projects are textile-based, while other projects involve basket-weaving, wood or paper products, and jewellery.

ThaiCraft's activities include supporting community groups in order to help them move towards self-reliance, co-ordinating the activities of producers in order to ensure fair payment, and maximising marketing opportunities to increase producers' income. A further objective is to provide training for producers to increase their knowledge and capabilities in product design, production techniques, efficient organisation, and marketing skills. ThaiCraft states that it is also concerned with preserving its producers' communities, traditions, culture, and environment (ThaiCraft 1997).

ThaiCraft works with a number of smaller grassroots projects and NGOs within Thailand, with foreign donors and agencies such as the British Government's Department for International Development (DFID), and other NGOs such as Oxfam, or Traidcraft. These organisations provide financial or technical support: for example, Traidcraft sent British-based designers to Thailand to run workshops to advise producers on design, materials, quality control, marketing, and fashion (Report of

ThaiCraft Producers' Workshop 1994). These organisations also purchase ThaiCraft products for sale in the UK. However, most ThaiCraft products are sold at large sales in Bangkok, aimed directly at (and very popular with) the expatriate community. Over 1,500 customers attended ThaiCraft's May 1997 sale, and total sales volume in 1996-97 raised Baht 11,098,904 (approximately £264,000), contributing to a surplus of Baht 367,032 (approximately £8,700) — a significant achievement (ThaiCraft 1997).

Some of the NGO projects which Thai-Craft supports could be classified as redemptive or protective in nature: the Good Shepherd sisters in Nong Khai runs a weaving co-operative for young women; the Padang Coconut project on the Malaysian border with employs young women and some men, many of whom have been previously involved in drugs smuggling (ThaiCraft 1997); and the White Lotus project, set up by Thammasat University for 'young women in high prostitution risk areas of Chiang Mai' (Kind 1994, 7). A ThaiCraft press release explicitly states that '... ThaiCraft supports efforts to provide alternative income possibilities to communities, thus lessening the need for urban migration, prostitution and environmental destruction' (Report of ThaiCraft Producers' Workshop 1994: Appendix E). On the back of the organisation's 1997 Christmas card, it reiterates this commitment: 'By nurturing their own traditional handicrafts, artisans can earn a sustainable income at home and choose to avoid the alternative of urban migration.'

Providing alternative paid employment in this way is widely perceived as important and valuable, (and particularly so in the current climate of growing awareness of the risk of HIV infection among migrant sex workers). The negative perceptions of the social and moral consequences of female migration are well documented throughout Asia (Buang 1993,

198), but in Thailand, little distinction seems to be made in terms of village perceptions, between those women who are factory labourers and those who become prostitutes. The moral stigma attached to female migrants makes them unpopular as brides, and those known to have worked as prostitutes may find themselves unwelcome in their village (Skrobanek, Boonpakdi, and Janthakeero 1997).

However, participating in craft-based NGO activities needs to be seen in context. Should existing markets collapse, then young women producers, with their lack of recognised skills and formal qualifications, have few choices open to them other than migration to urban areas. It therefore makes sense for such projects to equip participants with recognised skills which can be adapted to meet the changing demands of the employment market, and to challenge stereotypes of the kinds of skills required for weaving. However, as the following sections will suggest, traditional values associated with 'good weavers', 'good women', and the home, tend to be reified through such projects. This can be seen as an essentially conservative agenda, which fails to develop women's technological skills into new areas, and at the same time fails to challenge gender stereotypes of women by raising awareness of those mathematical, technical, scientific, and artistic skills they already possess.

Women's skills and attributes in traditional textile production

One reason for the popularity of textile and craft-based NGO projects may be that such projects are seen as suitable for women, building on their perceived natural skills such as manual dexterity and great patience. However, traditional cloth-production skills are much more complex and technical than this; while at times it may be a time-consuming, tedious, and repetitive procedure, involving patience as well as manual dexterity, it also requires great mathematical, technical, scientific (Harris 1997) and artistic skills, as shown in Table 1 below. In addition, the skills required are not natural, but learned at home from childhood, passed on from mother to daughter.

In north and north-east Thailand, weaving is strongly associated with 'womanly virtues' (Conway 1992), and the production process itself is value-laden in terms of a woman's or girl's status in the village. The relationship between weaving and success as a wife is clearly recognised in traditional village societies, where young women known to possess the technical skills of weaving are prized as future brides as illustrated by the following village saying: 'A good wife is like a ploughshare. If she is skilled at weaving then her husband can wear fine clothes. A wife who talks harshly and is unskilled at her loom makes a family poor and shabby in dress' (Conway 1992, 42).

In the past, young men would court their future wives as the girls spun or wove cloth. Weaving terms make up metaphors for physical and romantic love, as shown in this example which would be sung to a young woman by her suitor: 'You are to be compared to the finest silk cloth and the most delicate silk thread. You are as cool and as beautiful as silk. I wish I had thread for you to weave, but I do not know if you are interested in me or if you think I am an undyed inferior yarn. Please do not think of me that way but put my thread in your loom'. (Conway 1992, 44).

The moral associations of textiles and virtuous women seem to have been internalised to some degree by ThaiCraft. ThaiCraft encourages its volunteers to visit villages and meet its producers. After one such visit, an expatriate volunteer reported: 'Patience is the main virtue needed, and sadly many of the present generation of young women prefer other areas of employment ...' (ThaiCraft, March 1998). Patience is perceived as a natural feminine virtue here (echoing the case of female factory workers, discussed in the next section), and there is an implied slur on those young women who prefer other areas of employment. Such views are ironic when expressed by expatriates, many of whom are in Thailand in connection with the very industries and businesses which encourage urban migration, and are engaged in a global economy which attributes little value — moral, cultural, artistic, or economic — to traditional crafts and craft skills.

Table 1: Skills required for traditional cloth production in north and north-east Thailand

Mathematical skills	Technical and scientific skills	Artistic skills
Practical knowledge of:	**Practical knowledge of:**	**Practical knowledge of:**
Geometrical and symmetrical properties of patterns	Lifecycle and care of silk worm and cotton plants	Designs and patterns
Measurements of cloth, loom, designs	Properties of natural and chemical dyes	Colours
Numbers of threads per pattern and cloth	Properties and limitations of the loom	
	Weaving and spinning	
	Colour mixing theory	
	Dyeing techniques	

Industrialisation, migration, and perceptions of skill

What is the situation of village women who are forced into urban migration through poverty? Skilled weavers who need to find work outside their village, will be classified as unskilled labourers, and accordingly have few employment opportunities open to them. There is a strong gender division of labour in traditional textile production in the villages of north and north-east Thailand. Hand-weaving and spinning are traditionally done exclusively by women, while men construct and maintain looms and spinning wheels and often count the threads before they are tied onto the looms (personal observation). Here, we see a division of labour where women's tasks are perceived as involving manual dexterity and men's as involving 'heavy' or 'technical' work. There is ample evidence, some of which is discussed here, that this traditional gender division of labour continues in industrial settings.

Over the past 30 years, Thailand has prioritised industrialisation, particularly export-oriented industrialisation; the textiles, garments, and electronics industries have become the largest contributors to Gross Domestic Product (GDP) and exports. As a result, migration from rural to urban areas has increased dramatically. Female migrants now exceed male: twice as many women as men aged 11-19 migrate to Bangkok — not least because of the preference for cheap female labour in the garments, textile and electronics industries (Sainsbury 1997).

The reasons why young female labour is so attractive to these industries has been extensively discussed elsewhere (Elson and Pearson 1981, Mitter 1986, and others). Briefly summarised, women are perceived to be innately docile and patient, able to undertake repetitive tedious tasks without complaint, and to have naturally 'nimble fingers' which enable them to quickly complete intricate and delicate tasks such as the construction of garments, electronic circuit boards, or computer parts. A 1991 study of the largely migrant female work-force of an American electrical factory in Thailand showed that the beliefs outlined above were still prevalent among management. In particular, 'small but skilful hands, and dexterity' were named as necessary attributes for manipulating the minuscule components (Charoenloet, Soonthorndhada, and Saiprasert 1991, 15). Because these skills — having been learned at home — are seen as natural, or otherwise as 'non-skills', women's work is perceived as unskilled, and women can be paid very low wages for their labour. In addition, they are also required to work long hours, often in poor conditions. It is this low pay, combined with the perception of women as unskilled, which makes prostitution one of the few channels open to women who wish to make more substantial sums of money quickly (Archavanitkul in Skrobanek, Boonpakdi, and Janthakeero 1997).

Constructing 'skills' and 'non-skills'

While the 'nimble fingers' argument provides an explanation for why industries are keen to recruit young Thai women, women's identities and skills are in fact constructed in different ways in Thailand, depending on time and location. In the village setting, as we have seen, proficiency in weaving and cloth production in the village and domestic sphere is imbued with great value, and indicates the possession of womanly virtues and marriageability. Yet in the industrial sphere, the same skills are seen as non-skills, and employment in industries utilising these non-skills actually detracts from a woman's virtue and marriageability. Having lived and worked outside the patriarchal control of the parental home, young women are perceived as morally and sexually suspect.

This idea is reinforced by 'redemptive' textile and craft projects which attempt to 'save' women from the social stigma of urbanisation, and return them to the patriarchal control of working at home.

It is important to note here that traditional textile production is done at home, often by female relatives working together. This means that reproductive labour, such as child-care, cooking and washing, can be done at the same time as productive labour, such as weaving. It also means that young women's virtue can be guaranteed, as there is no need for them to leave the household, and they will have little financial independence. Many female factory workers say increased freedom and financial independence is one of the benefits of factory labour (Sainsbury 1997), but it is this very freedom which engenders suspicion about their morals . Indeed, one reason for the popularity of craft-based NGO projects with local communities as well as donors (Harris 1997) is that single women involved in the projects usually work at home, or at least in their village, where traditional patriarchal structures can be maintained. In addition, the idea of the male as wage earner is not challenged because if women work at home, or at least in their village, their work can be identified as 'non-skilled' non-work, because it is women's work (Lever 1988). The relationship between perceptions of women's skills, and how these are addressed in NGO education and training programmes will be examined in more detail in the next section.

NGOs, skills training, and education

One of ThaiCraft's aims is to 'form dynamic educational partnerships among producers, volunteers and the public' (ThaiCraft 1997, 4). I interpret this to mean attempting to raise the profile of crafts, and of producers and their technological skills. This could be extremely valuable in the process of deconstructing and reconstructing perceptions of craft skills, and women's craft skills in particular. Gaskell has argued that notions of skill are constructed through social conventions and ideologies, and that the discourse of skills is the discourse of power. Skills designations are used to confer status and importance on some kinds of work, and remove it from others (Gaskell 1995).

Visible training programmes leading to recognised qualifications could help in recognising and valuing women's skills and women's work. However, many craft-based NGO projects are based on the assumption that producers already possess the ability to sew, weave, embroider, paint, and dye, and little or no training is given in these areas. In ThaiCraft projects, some training is given in non-traditional areas: in basket weaving for men, and in pattern-cutting for women and men, as required, because this is largely pattern-cutting for western styles which neither women nor men will be familiar with.

Neither are the existing technical, mathematical and scientific skills of women craft producers recognised and promoted in publicity and marketing material, which concentrates instead on publicising their manual dexterity and patience. Thus, in the name of preserving traditional communities, cultures, and crafts, craft-based NGO projects can be seen as perpetuating images of women as number-fingered passive workers: effectively training them for low-paid factory work.

ThaiCraft, like other craft-based projects, does provide training opportunities for producers to strengthen their knowledge and capabilities in design, production techniques, and efficient organisation and marketing skills. ThaiCraft achieves this through on-site training sessions with producers and regional or national workshops (Report of ThaiCraft 1994 Producer's Workshop). Similarly, in 1997 a British designer worked with six trainees in

Buriram to improve design, sizing, finishing, and choice of cloth for a new range of natural-look clothing (ThaiCraft 1997). The training in these particular skills is extremely worthwhile in itself and transferable to other types of work. However, in common with many other such craft-based NGOs, ThaiCraft does not currently involve itself in providing opportunities, or encouraging producers, to gain a formal education or qualifications. If some producers were to gain artistic, business, or marketing qualifications, this would also raise the profile of their work and potentially provide greater employment opportunities in the future.

Conclusion

The question remains as to whether craft-based NGOs, and other organisations which build on skills perceived as 'womanly' and naturally acquired, can really provide a viable long-term alternative to urban migration. Not only do these activities employ relatively small numbers of women, but critics argue that textile projects can create 'further ghettos for women, keeping them outside "mainstream" development' (Harris 1997, 203). At present, should the craft enterprises encouraged by ThaiCraft and other such organisations fail — which, given the fickleness of their markets is not unlikely — the women involved will still have few employment opportunities open to them other than urban migration, factory work or prostitution, as they will be perceived as unskilled outside the village context. While such projects set out to fight gender inequalities and reduce the exploitation of women, it can be argued that at best, they delay urban migration, and often do little more than hone women's skills for poorly paid, insecure work. In addition, they help to maintain traditional patriarchal value distinctions between women who weave and women who migrate, and perpetuate patriarchal structures by encouraging women to do home-based work (Lever 1988).

There is a need for a revaluation of women's traditional areas of work (Gaskell 1995). In my view, the most valuable area of work of organisations such as ThaiCraft is in promoting traditional crafts such as weaving, and in promoting craft producers' skills, as these are essentially associated with women. However, craft-based NGOs need to take their business, marketing and design training programmes further, encouraging participants to develop new skills and build on existing ones, and where possible to take formal qualifications, so that their talents and skills may be more easily recognised.

If NGOs fail to challenge traditional gender stereotypes at the local level, then there is little hope that it can be done at the level of export industries, where women undertake intricate production and assembly procedures while men carry out maintenance and pre-assembly work, and are far more likely to work with machinery and technology than women (Sainsbury 1997). These divisions not only result in differential pay and conditions based on gender, but also differential training, and promotion and future employment chances. NGOs could do much more to challenge the traditional gender division of labour in their projects, and to re-evaluate women's traditional craft skills. At the same time, NGOs should make more of the scientific, technical and mathematical skills involved in crafts such as textile production, while preserving traditional arts and crafts.

Solutions suggested here cannot respond to all the issues faced by young rural Thai women who migrate to urban areas for employment as factory workers or in the sex industry; however, the recognition of women's skills and knowledge is at the heart of the fight against gender inequality in development.

Rachel Humphreys spent a year working in Thailand and was able to carry out research into women in textile production. She now teaches at the School of Oriental and African Studies, Thornhaugh St, Russell Square, London WC1H 0XG; e-mail: rh7@soas.ac.uk

References

Buang, A (1993) 'Development and Factory Women: Negative Perceptions from a Malaysian Source Area', in Momsen, JH and Kinnaird, V (eds.) *Different Places, Different Voices: Gender and Development in Africa, Asia and Latin America*, Routledge, London.

Charoenloet, V, Soonthorndhada, A, and Saiprasert, S (1991) 'Factory management, skill formation and attitudes of women workers in Thailand: A comparison between an American-owned electrical factory and a Japanese-owned electrical factory', Institute for Population and Social Research, Mahidol University, Bangkok.

Conway, S (1992) *Thai Textiles*, British Museum Press, London.

Elson, D and Pearson, R (1981) 'Nimble Fingers Make Cheap Workers: An Analysis of Women's Employment in Third World Export Manufacturing', in *Feminist Review*, No. 7, Spring 1981.

Gaskell, J (1995) 'Gender and the School Work Transition in Canada and the USA', in Bash, L and Green, A (eds.) *World Yearbook of Education (1995)*, Kogan Page, London and Philadelphia.

Harris, M (1997) *Common Threads: Women, Mathematics and Work*, Trentham Books, Staffordshire.

Kind, S (1994) 'Environmentally Friendly Fashion', *Bangkok Post*, 27 October 1994.

Lever, A (1988) 'Capital, Gender and Skill: Women Homeworkers in Rural Spain', in *Feminist Review* No. 30, Autumn 1988.

Mitter, S (1986) *Common Fate Common Bond: Women in the Global Economy*, Pluto Press, London.

Sainsbury, J (1997) *The New Inequality: Women Workers' Lives in Thailand and the Philippines*, CIIR, London.

Skrobanek, S, Boonpakdi, N, Janthakeero, C (1997) *The Traffic in Women: Human Realities of the International Sex Trade*, Zed Books, London.

ThaiCraft (1994) *ThaiCraft Hands November 1994*, The ThaiCraft Association, Bangkok.

ThaiCraft (1994) Report of ThaiCraft 1994 Producers' Workshop, The ThaiCraft Association, Bangkok.

ThaiCraft (1995) 'A Direction for the Future from the Manager's Viewpoint', The ThaiCraft Association, Bangkok.

ThaiCraft (1997) ThaiCraft Annual Report 1996-7, The ThaiCraft Association, Bangkok.

ThaiCraft (1998) *ThaiCraft*, Vol. 5, Issue 2, The ThaiCraft Association, Bangkok.

ThaiCraft (1998), *ThaiCraft News*, 25 April 1998, The ThaiCraft Association, Bangkok.

Rural women, development, and telecommunications:

A pilot programme in South Africa

Heather Schreiner

Telecentres — places where people can pay for the use of devices such as telephones, fax machines, and computers — are currently opening throughout Africa. They are seen as providing a much-needed communications infrastructure to a continent poorly supplied by telecomunication facilities (Acacia 1997). Heather Schreiner outlines the obstacles to rural women gaining from this technology.

The South African government's 1995 Telecommunication Policy Green Paper set out to promote telecommunication and information access to all South Africans. In 1997, the Universal Service Agency (USA), a statutory body, was established in accordance with the Telecommunications Act (103 of 1996). The agency committed itself to a programme of creating 'information literacy for all' (USA 1996). Its primary focus was to promote access to telecommunications for all in South Africa, by co-ordinating a pilot programme of ten telecentre sites in rural 'disadvantaged areas'. Community groups throughout South Africa were requested to tender for the telecentres. In the following, I will describe how the community of Bamshela in rural KwaZulu/Natal has used its telecentre as a resource since its opening in 1998.

The development research project in KwaZulu/Natal

Rural women continue to be disenfranchised in the new democratic South Africa through the lasting male control over social and economic affairs. Lack of education, poverty, and lack of access to information were preventing women from getting vital resources to support development and capacity-building activities in rural areas. Thus, the telecentre initiative seemed innovative and potentially rewarding to women. The possibility of universal access to telecommunication and information resources, which could support and enhance many agricultural, health, and education initiatives currently available for women, seemed to be a step in the right direction.

This article draws on evidence collected in the course of my research into the telecentre in Bamshela, Kwa-Zulu, and its impact on women and men in the local community. My involvement began two months before the telecentre opened on 29 April 1998, and will conclude in April 2000. I employ an 'active research' approach through regular visits to the telecentre for discussions, observation, and interviews. The aim of this 'hands-on' approach has been to gain insight into the early stages of the telecentre development and contribute positively towards the development by advising on service provision and hardware maintenance, and by networking with associated agencies. In the course of my research, managers are interviewed approximately every six weeks, while clients, and women and men from the local community, are interviewed when possible. The telecentre managers actively engage as interpreters whenever and wherever possible. I also participate in the development of the telecentre by contacting and 'networking' with agencies on behalf of the telecentre (for example locating telephone directories and affordable photocopying paper), and encouraging visits by potential funders and interested professionals.

The context in Bamshela

Bamshela is a busy crossroads, at the confluence of three tribal areas. A supermarket, refreshment outlet, and taxi ranks, as well as the new telecentre, provide services to the local community as well as to travellers going north to Richards Bay and the Mozambican border, and south to Pietermaritzburg, the capital of KwaZulu/Natal, and to the busy Indian Ocean port of Durban. Bamshela is a predominantly Zulu, clan-based, agrarian community, organised and overseen by the local headmen and Induna (chief).

Bamshela is very fortunate in having a number of active civic groups, who exchange information and resources through their strong community structures. The Arts and Culture committee, along with the Water and Amenities Committees are democratic bodies established by parts of the local community to engage with government agencies and lobby for the provision of services; it was the Arts and Culture committee at Bamshela which submitted the successful tender to the government for the telecentre. The violent clashes between supporters of political parties that have been so prevalent in other areas of KwaZulu/Natal have not occurred in Bamshela, which many attribute to the overwhelming support for the Inkatha

Freedom Party in the region (discussions with members of the Arts and Culture committee, Bamshela,1998). Inkatha is culturally and socially posited within the Zulu tradition, and since Bamshela has a strongly Zulu identity, the ANC ruling party has very little influence in this region. Managers of the telecentre told me that they thought Bamshela could again be spared any political violence during the national elections in June 1999 (discussions, 1998-99).

Bamshela is typical of a rural South African district: unemployment is high, basic infrastructure of water and electricity is not comprehensively available. Local roads are not tar-sealed, and most *kraals* (homesteads) have no vehicle access. Most families are engaged in subsistence farming; any cash coming in to the community is generated by family members working as migrant labour in Durban and Richards Bay, or further afield in the northern mining areas. There is no major industry in Bamshela; farming employs the largest number of people. There are 40 schools in the district, none of which have computer facilities. Until 1998, there were no public phones available in the district.

Women in Bamshela spend their lives engaged in subsistence farming and perhaps some small-scale income-generating activities. They spend up to six hours each day collecting water and fuel. In many respects, their lives have not changed from those of women generations before: the closest they may ever come to a telecommunication resource is to witness the local shop owner using a telephone or cash register. During the course of my research, I was fascinated by the apparent collision between two very different cultures: that of agrarian technologists (rural women), and that of the information and communications technologies (ICT) professionals behind yahoo.com. What would rural women make of the telecentre? Would such a resource at Bamshela contribute in any way to meaningful change for rural women?

The conception of the Government's telecentre initiative included awareness of gender issues and the need to promote women's needs and rights. Each telecentre site had to employ at least one woman as a trained manager (USA 1996). A local telecentre clearly has the potential to enhance rural women's access to much-needed telecommunication and information resources, and to enable capacity-building to take place. A number of government and non-government bodies have been encouraging South African women to develop computing and information technology (IT) skills in order to be become part of the expanding IT employment market. These include the Gender Commission, a government body set up to monitor and review the status of women with regards to the 1996 Constitution of South Africa; SANGoNET, a not-for-profit Internet service provider; and Women's Net, also a not-for-profit Internet service provider. A recent report submitted to the Gender and Sustainable Development Unit, states that 'the promotion of education and training initiatives' targeting women as potential users and facilitators, and 'supporting the implementation of ICT access' by women, would facilitate 'access to electronic information as a trans-formation tool'. (Huyer 1997).

The telecentre's first year

From the start, many in the Bamshela community were excited by the prospect of being awarded a telecentre, and expectations for such a local resource were high (discussions with community members, 1998). Not only was the centre likely to be a useful communication resource, but the community was aware of the potential of the centre for development, education, and training. They recognised the potential of the site to attract and encourage the growth of new small business enterprises in the community.

Bamshela, and the other nine pilot sites, were awarded the same model of tele-centre, of which details are given below. It was planned that each centre would be able to adapt and evolve their hardware to the community requirements it serviced. It was envisaged that the telecentres would provide not only much-needed public telephone access, but also faxing facilities, photocopying, poster printing, scanning, CV composition, skills training and distance-learning facilities. Government funding, with donor support, picked up the bill for the pilot projects, and paid for site renovation and building, basic training, and service support for 12 months after opening. It was expected that each centre would work as a small business enterprise. Clients would pay for the use of telephone and fax, photocopying, computing, e-mail and Internet facilities, at a rate that would generate income for the telecentre (USA 1996). It was predicted that this income would allow the telecentre to become economically viable after a year, and that any profits would be re-invested in the telecentres to upgrade and develop resources (USA 1996).

Work on building and renovating the site for Bamshela's telecentre, and the selection and training of two members of the community to be locally-based managers, began in 1997. The telecentre is located in a converted health clinic next to the town's bottle store and building suppliers. The centre opened in April 1998, to much fanfare and celebration. USA had opened the first telecentre in KwaZulu/ Natal on time, and to date, it is the only one in Natal that is fully operational. There were six telephone lines with headsets, a fax machine, a photocopier, six state-of-the-art Pentium computers, and a scanner. The two managers (one of whom was a woman) had been trained in computing and management skills. However, the managers said that they considered their three-week period of basic training to have been inadequate, and state that the promised support and back-up facilities had not been provided (interviews, 1998-99).

Setbacks and challenges

At the time of writing (May 1999), as the centre moves into its second year, there are indications that many opportunities for the telecentre to make a meaningful impact on the community from the start have been lost. The Internet facility was only success-fully installed by the telecentre's first birthday. The printer stopped working after the first day, and until April 1999 managers have had to undertake a five-hour journey to print at a different facility, because they have been unable to raise enough capital from the telecentre income to buy a new printer. The Arts and Culture Committee has now made a loan available to pay for a new printer, and managers say that this has made a great difference to the centre's ability to provide a comprehensive service (ibid.). Two of the computers are used to produce basic resumes for clients who can pay. Assistants from the community have been trained to help with this task, and the managers say that they hope to train more assistants to develop areas such as website design, scanning, and e-mail and Internet usage (ibid.).

Managers told me in March 1998 that, in the current situation, they cannot develop their roles as they had hoped at the time of their training. They had aimed to be resource managers and educators for the community. One year down the line, they have been forced to become more realistic. There is no longer talk of imminent plans for literacy and business-skills training for local women's groups. Time and money that could have been spent training local women and men how to register e-mail addresses, create web-sites to advertise their products, and network with other groups nationally and internationally, is taken up with looking for other sources of

income to the centre. The telecentre has begun to work on an application to the regional library service for the placement of a library facility at the centre, which would provide a wider range of resources on one site and generate further sales (ibid.).

Managers are frustrated because they cannot realise and utilise all the facilities that are housed in their centre. It was projected that employment opportunities at the centre would grow as the facilities come on line and develop, but this has not proved possible, beyond the fact that an additional three male managers have been employed. Managers also report that they are unable to train others because of their own lack of knowledge. They do not know what will happen to the computers after 2000, or whether they will have enough money to upgrade. Managers' concerns about security force them to sleep at the centre, and often the trainee staff act as security guards at night, with the result that, thus far, the telecentre has had no robberies (interview, March 1999).

The telecentre cannot as yet generate enough income to keep prices at an affordable rate for all. The telephone service has been, unexpectedly, the largest source of revenue, due to the problems with the other facilities. Yet the revenue realised by the phones is not sufficient to ensure financial security. Problems with one telephone line have not been resolved and it continues to give problems, as it did from day one. More importantly, telephone lines at Bamshela are vulnerable to local weather conditions, and frequent break-downs mean that much-needed revenue is lost. At the time of writing, the telecentre borrows electricity from the generator of the bottle store next door when its own system breaks down (interviews, 1998-9).

By March 1999, prices for all the facilities had increased by 150 per cent since opening, from 40 cents per phone call unit to one Rand per unit. (exchange rate is currently R10.00:£1.00, and, according to discussions with community members in 1999, monthly earnings in Bamshela are in the range of R700 to R1,300). Many people in Bamshela, especially women, feel that economic factors exclude them from using the centre's resources (interviews, 1999). The telecentre managers fear that what began as a potential income-generating resource will very shortly become a financial burden to the community, which the local Arts and Culture Committee would have to shoulder. Although the telecentre was funded and supported by the government for one year, the income generated by the centre is now supposed to pay for its upkeep, wages, and services. It is a resource that is owned by the community.

Since its opening, the telecentre has declined as a popular meeting place; managers clearly have an uphill task in encouraging the community to reclaim the centre for themselves, and to be interested in what it has to offer. The centre plans an advertising campaign in Bamshela to re-generate local interest: it is encouraging customers to use the Internet to view their names on the voters' register prior to the national elections on 2 June 1999.

The impact on women

The telecentre now employs five staff, but only one of these is a woman, responsible for 'customer services'. Although she has been trained in business management and computer skills, she does not use those skills in her current position. When asked about this she said she enjoys her work as it is, but feels that she needs more training to provide a wider range of services, because she has not been using many of her computer skills in the past year (personal communication, 1999).

From my research, it seems clear that many women from the Bamshela commu-nity are using the telecentre as a phone shop. During interviews with passers-by undertaken in April 1999, women were asked if they had ever used the telecentre. Half of them said that they used the facility to telephone friends and relatives, when they had spare money and were near the telecentre. A straw poll at the telecentre showed that over 70 per cent of customers using any facility, and 60 per cent of customers using the telephone, are women. The average amount spent on a phone call in the telecentre is R5. Ninety per cent of requests for CV writing come from women, and half the students requesting computer time are female.

Changes to gender relations may come about as a result of using the telephone. The ease of communication with family members working as migrant workers appears to have led to some changes in budgeting arrangements. Interviews with women whose husbands work as migrant workers confirmed that they now budget their income in consultation with their husbands over the phone.

The telephone is a useful communication tool for families forced to live apart for long periods of time. According to the telecentre managers, women who live in more isolated communities far away from the telecentre usually travel together by taxi to the telecentre at weekends. It is still quite a novelty to them, and the calls are expensive: women indicated that there are times when telephone money is used to buy more important necessities, like food and schoolbooks. Telecentre records show that the average call made to keep in touch with family is about R30.[1]

The women customers I have inter-viewed cited their lack of language skills and education as an obstacle to computer use: the meeting between cultures I had wished to witness does not appear to have yet happened. As stated earlier, so far there have been no skills-training programmes available to them. In my view, telling women about the use of ICT, and providing training, would not be enough in any case to promote their sustained use of new technology. Apart from telephone usage, women's lives do not as yet require them to use other telecentre services. Unless women see practical and immediate benefits, it seems likely that they will continue as passive observers of the other technologies on offer at the telecentre.

However, the managers of the telecentre believe that rural women will become familiar with electronic methods of communications, and may come to use services at the telecentre (discussions, 1998-99). It is true that changes are coming fast: as rural women become more familiar with telephone use, they are also experiencing greater exposure to ICTs through their daily activities around the home. A growing number of homes in Bamshela have electricity and more households are purchasing televisions, electric stoves, microwaves, and cell phones. More businesses are moving into Bamshela as it expands; banks and other commercial enterprises may arrive in the future. It is through using goods and services such as these that a desire to actively engage with ICT will come about.

In an interview in April 1999 with women using the telephone facility at the telecentre, it was suggested that ITC could be used to market their products and make contact with other women to share ideas to enhance the selling potential. The women said that this would not meet their needs, since leaving the home environment was what they looked forward to, and any money they made in the process was helpful but not as important as getting away from the home for the day. In the market place in the urban centres of Stanger and Durban, they can meet friends as well as sell their products, and it is through these face-to-face contacts that the all-important communication and information transfer is carried out. The women told me that sharing information on grants and government initiatives, health developments, farming innovations, community gossip and such like.

The telecentre has a long way to go before it can replace face-to-face communication. To my knowledge, no rural women's organisations tendered for one of the pilot telecentres in 1997, and to date there are no women's groups currently managing these centres in South Africa. The women in Bamshela are very happy that the centre is in their community. Opinion canvassed from women who use the telecentre shows that most of them are optimistic that the centre will continue and will be a valuable resource for their children, which brings prestige to the community. 'This centre is very good for us. Many people have come here,' a woman from Bamshela told me. 'It is good for the students to use the computers. It helps them to understand what goes on'. I asked her if she had used the computers. She laughed, pointing to the valley, and looked at her hands. 'I am too busy out there. I do not have the eyes of the students, and my hands make pots'. As yet, it seems that most women do not need to collide with Yahoo.com.

Heather Schreiner is a writer and researcher of gender issues. She can be contacted at: PO Box 1362, Hilton 3245, KwaZulu/Natal, South Africa. E-mail: d.schreiner@pixie.co.za

Notes

1 It should be noted that the telecentre records, while giving an indication of use, are not an accurate and comprehensive source due to inconsistent use by the managers. A challenge of my research has been to find a workable system of record-keeping for the managers in the second year of the telecentre.

References

Acacia, IDRC (1997) 'Communities and the Information Society in Africa: Challenging Objectives', Government of

South Africa, Department of Communication.
Web site: www.doc.gov.sa

Government of South Africa (1996) Telecommunication Act.

Government of South Africa(1995) Telecommunication Policy Green Paper.

Huyer, S (1997) 'Supporting Women's Use of Information Technologies for Sustainable Development', paper submitted to the Gender and Sustainable Development Unit, IDRC, 18 February 1997.

Schreiner, HDR (1997) 'Participatory Communication Strategies for women in an emerging democracy', BA (Hons) dissertation, University of Natal.

Universal Service Agency, Telecentre Project (1996) 'Telecentre selection criteria and application form', information pamphlet. Web site: www.usa.org.za/projects/teleformhtml

The denigration of women in Malawian radio commercials

Charles Chilimampunga

A sample of 100 commercials aired on Malawian radio showed that many use messages which denigrate women, who are represented as voices of little authority, non-competitive, dependent, attention-seeking, and confined to the domestic sphere. Such commercials perpetuate women's subordination, and hinder their full participation in development.

The Malawi Broadcasting Corporation (MBC) runs the main radio station in Malawi. Recently, this organisation aired a commercial which referred to housewives as 'women who just sit at home' (personal observation, 1997). This implies that the work of caring for home and family, which most Malawian women do daily, is not work at all. This is just one example of the negative stereotypes peppering our radio advertising. While mass communications technologies can be used positively for development, they can also contribute to women's subordination. In particular, advertising in the mass media has been shown in studies outside Malawi to portray females as dependent, non-competitive, and home-oriented, with little authority (Goffman 1979, Posner 1987, Singer 1986). Women tend to be shown in their 'traditional' gender roles: as either housewives, whose interests are limited to domestic needs, or as a sexually alluring 'background' to advertisements, making the advertised goods attractive by association.

This paper is based on a study in which I examined a random sample of 100 commercials of various products and services, which were aired on MBC Radio 1 over a one-week period. This study aimed to find out the extent to which women in Malawi are denigrated in radio commercials, to examine how media images of women are created, and to suggest some ways of reducing the extent of women's denigration. Radio commercials which ridicule or condemn women make it hard for women to assert their personal identity, to break down gender stereotypes, and to enjoy freedom. Other commercials do not convey negative images of women, choosing instead to focus on men. It is my contention that in a male-dominated society, such absence of women's issues is tantamount to supporting women's subordination.

Methodology

The 100 commercials were tape-recorded, transcribed, and analysed using the method of content analysis. For each sex, five pairs of images (one negative and the other positive) were constructed. Each commercial was examined to see whether it was 'gender-neutral', or whether it presented females and males as people who have little or much authority; who are dependent or independent; home-oriented or office-oriented; non-competitive or competitive; and who are seen as 'sex-objects' or as 'complete individuals'. It must be noted that while home-orientation and office-orientation in themselves are neither negative nor positive images, Malawian society regards the former as negative, mostly because of its association with low monetary rewards.

Presentation of gender in radio commercials

Table 1 shows, for each sex, the number of commercials which portrayed one of the ten images. Females were portrayed negatively more often than males: for example, almost 80 per cent of commercials portrayed men as having authority, compared to only 13 per cent of women.

Table 2 summarises the portrayal of both the male and female character(s) appearing in a particular commercial. Only seven of the 100 commercials mentioned neither women nor men. Females were portrayed positively in just seven commercials, while males had a positive image in 77 of them. While only three commercials presented males in a purely negative way, 27 presented females in this way. Of those

which were silent on females (more than half of the sample), 48 commercials portrayed males positively, while of those silent on males, only five portrayed females positively. Commercials which contained assertions of male superiority were deemed to be denigrating women indirectly.

Poor representation of females in commercials

The sex of the character(s) voicing or airing each of the 100 commercials was discerned from their voices, names, and titles. A female voice was heard in fewer than half of the 100 commercials, while a male voice was heard in as many as 91 of them (see Table 3). In addition, 53 commercials featured a male voice only, compared to nine which featured females only.

A questionnaire was sent to MBC management in 1995, and their responses pointed towards a number of factors which appear to influence the poor numerical representation of women in radio commercials. First, management reported that this reflects the poor representation of females on the MBC staff: only 11.4 per cent are women (Kaimila-Kanjo 1995, 4). Fewer than 40 per cent of MBC employees who read out commercials on radio, or record them, are female. Second, MBC managers reported that advertisers think that women lack the expertise to sell products and services on the radio, and consider radio

Table 1: Number of commercials by gender and image portrayed

Negative image	Gender		Positive image	Gender	
	Female	Male		Female	Male
Little authority	24	5	Much authority	13	78
Dependent	4	2	Independent	2	26
Home-oriented	8	2	Office-oriented	4	12
Non-competitive	5	0	Competitive	0	5
Sex objects	4	1	Complete individuals	7	56

Table 2: Portrayal of males and females in the 100 commercials assessed

		Females				
	Image	**Negative**	**Silent**	**Pos/Neg**	**Positive**	**Total**
Males	Negative	0	0	2	1	3
	Silent	0	7	3	5	15
	Pos / Neg	2	2	1	0	5
	Positive	25	48	3	1	77
	Total	27	57	9	7	100

commercials to be less effective when they are voiced or aired by a female. This is borne out by the fact that clients who submit ready-made commercials use the male voice most frequently. MBC managers confirmed that clients often demand that their commercials are read on air by men.

Third, where the client leaves MBC to choose the person to voice a commercial, MBC uses voices it deems suitable to the type of commercial. Staff reported to me that they make an effort to relate the content of a commercial to the sex of the person who will voice it. This suggests that staff at MBC view the content of most of the commercials as suitable to be voiced by men, although I as researcher strongly hold the view that all the advertisements could have been aired by either sex. Finally, I was told by radio staff that, having voiced a commercial, women have been known to later withdraw their voices from the commercial, because of negative stereo-

types associated with the selling of some products and services (discussion with MBC manager, 1995).

Negative images of women

As Table 2 showed, 36 of the 100 commercials portrayed females negatively. Table 1 showed that 24 out of the 41 commercials which were judged to denigrate females presented the females as voices of little authority. Of the others, four showed them as dependent, eight as home-oriented, five as non-competitive people, and four as sex objects.

Women as voices of little authority
Some commercials suggest that women have very little authority. The males speak with a commanding tone of voice, and literally have the last word in many commercials. As Table 3 shows, a female

Table 3: Number of commercials by sex of all voices heard and sex of final voice(s) heard

Gender of all voices heard

Sex of final voice(s) heard	Female only	Female and Male	Male only	Total
Female only	9	5	0	14
Female and male	0	8	0	8
Male only	0	25	53	78
Total	9	38	53	100

was the last speaker in only 14 per cent of the commercials, whereas a male spoke last in 78 per cent of them. In commercials featuring female and male voices, the last voice heard was that of a female and a male in 13 per cent and 66 per cent of the commercials respectively. This finding reflects the observation that when women and men are in the same group, the men actually dominate the conversation and talk more than the women do. Further, men tend to interrupt women when they are speaking more than women interrupt men, as a show of power (Henley 1977, Tannen 1991). A sample of the 24 commercials suggesting that women have little authority is the following:

Commercial 1: Warm you up and refresh you (cosmetic)
   Female 1: Hi Jean! Oh, why the dry skin?
   Female 2: Well, Mary, I have tried all sort of oils …
   Female 1: Try the wonderful range of Care products, Jean…
   Female 2: Thank you for the advice, Mary.
   Male: Care Skin Beauty and Care Petroleum Jelly …

Here, the male speaks last in a conversation between two females. What he says could have been said by Female 1 or another female. The females' voices are muffled by the male's commanding tone of voice. (Of the 16 commercials about cosmetic products, 56 per cent were aired by, or featured conversations between, females only, 25 per cent by both females and males, and 19 per cent by males only.)

The dependency of women
Advertising encourages female dependency by urging women to be passive and not to live out their aspirations. In most of the commercials examined, a woman rarely makes decisions on her own, except where cooking and cosmetics are concerned. Even

in the above example, the male sets his seal on the woman's decision on cosmetics by endorsing the products (Kaimila-Kanjo 1995). In the next example, dealing with the serious issue of fertility, women's dependency on men's decision-making is unquestioned, and men are encouraged to take responsibility. The script has been translated into English from Chichewa.

Commercial 2: Teach your wife (family planning)
   Male 1: Child-spacing is your responsibility, father.
   Male 2: Most of us fathers know our family responsibilities. We mean to take care of our wives and children, to ensure that their daily needs are met…
   Male 1: Child-spacing is your responsibility, father.
   Male 2: As the husband and head of household, you should teach your wife about the importance of child-spacing if you are to manage to take care of your children, to fee, clothe and educate them without difficulties …
   Male 1: Child-spacing is your responsibility, father.

Although child-spacing is a responsibility which should be addressed jointly by both women and men, the woman is here deprived of power. She is portrayed as a passive wife and mother, waiting to be taught and cared for.

Confinement of women to the home
Of the 12 commercials which portray women in a particular setting or occupation, eight place the woman in the home, and only four portray her in occupations outside it. The women depicted working outside the home are a primary school teacher, a model/actress, a banker, and a nutritionist. Women are not portrayed in professional positions: as medical doctors, mechanics, professors, journalists, lawyers, and so on. Part of Commercial 3 implies that a woman's place is the home.

Commercial 3: 'Mums who know what's best cook in the best' (food product)

Female 1: How honest do you make your chicken taste …

Female 2: You know what …?

Female 1: Yes, mum!

Female 2: The only way your chicken …

Female 1: You promise mum?

Female 2: Ah! Have I ever told you wrongly, dear?

Female 1: Mums who know what's best, cook in the best. Even mothers and daughters agree.

Females: Covo, Malawi's favourite cooking oil.

Females and males sing: Covo!

The male in this commercial is simply waiting to be served the product of the females' labour. This reinforces the notion that cooking is a chore for females. While this commercial is reflecting the reality of the current gender division of labour in Malawi, and the Malawian tradition that cooking is a woman's task, using this stereotype in a commercial implies that this is how things 'ought' to be.

Many women are entering the labour market in Malawi: in 1990, 57 per cent were listed as own-account workers and 13 per cent as employees, while women have always formed a large part of the agricultural sector: 92 per cent are listed as farmers, compared to 63 per cent of men (UN 1995, 147). Yet advertisers continue to depict women as housewives and mothers, with housework and cookery as their only speciality and children as their only companion. It is true that 'women's entry into waged labour does not free them from their domestic responsibilities' (Rappoport and Rappoport 1978, 134). However, these responsibilities should not be emphasised at the expense of other occupations in which which women are engaged. The contributions women make to the success of both domestic and public spheres are equally important.

Non-competitive women

Only one out of the five commercials about sports studied features females. These advertisements emphasise sport as a way of motivating people to achieve, and channel their aggression. The fact that women are excluded from these commercials suggests that females are not seen as aggressive, but neither are they seen as motivated or achievement-oriented. Advertisers in Malawi seem to me to concur with Spock (quoted in Hobbs and Black 1975, 380-381) who asserts that 'women are designed to get pleasure out of life — when they are not aggressive — When they are encouraged to be competitive, too many of them become disagreeable.'

Commercial 4 suggests that females are not competitive. The females are mere spectators, gathered together to cheer their boy and his team to victory. The girls' giggling suggests that they need not be taken seriously.

Commercial 4: The boy with skills [translated from Chichewa]

Female 1: There are many boys playing the soccer game. Which of them do you like?

Female 2: There is only one. He is short, has dribbling skills and his uniform fits him perfectly well.

Female 1: (giggles) I know him. Shortcake! That's the one!

Male 1 (commentator): The ball is now with Shortcake, the short boy with dribbling skills

Female 1: You see! (giggles) Shortcake!

Male 2: Supporters call Highland Shortcake Biscuits 'the short boy with dribbling skills'.

Advertisers ignore the fact that many Malawian women have made great achievements in sports at national and international levels. For example, a netball team (the ADMARC Tigresses) won the Confederation of Southern African Netball

Associations trophy in 1992, a five-nation competition in which a Malawian girl was voted the best player. Examples of females who have made outstanding achievements abound in other professions. Since privileged groups seldom relinquish their privileges voluntarily, these women have motivated themselves to compete with men on equal terms.

Women as 'sex objects'

Mass communications technologies, including countless films and television as well as radio, are well-known for using women's sexual allure as alluring bait to draw in their audiences. Commercial radio uses this technique to capture listeners' attention and 'sell' products to potential buyers. Commercial 5 illustrates this technique:

Commercial 5: You'll love to see beauty in services in finance (financial services)

Female (seductively): FINCOM, Finance Corporation of Malawi Limited, your first choice in finance. We all love and like to see beautiful things, beautiful ideas, beautiful thoughts. We appreciate beauty in goodness, beauty in a silver lining of a cloud hanging in the sky. And when you come to FINCOM, you'll love and like to see the thick beauty embodied in the financial services offered. Come to FINCOM. You'll love to see beauty in our services in finance. You'll love to see beauty in our services in lending. You'll love to see beauty in our services in deposit-taking. Come to see beauty in FINCOM's services. Appreciate our services in finance. FINCOM, your first choice in finance.

In this advertisement, the words 'beauty' and 'beautiful' are used ten times, and 'love' five times. Seven of the ten sentences in the commercial contain at least one of these three words, although they are clearly

irrelevant to services in finance. A woman's voice is used, with a sensual tone, to attract listeners' attention and associate the product with female sexuality.

In sharp contrast, Commercial 6 also advertises financial services. Here, the advertiser suggests, through use of male voices and factual content, that the financial services offered are authoritative and trustworthy.

Commercial 6: Tailored with skill, precision, and perfection (financial services)

Male: Fixed deposits have long captivated businessmen, individuals, companies and corporations. With time, FINCOM, Finance Corporation of Malawi Limited, has tailored deposits with skill, precision and perfection to bring to its depositors the ultimate answer in providing extra kwachas through interest to cater for time of need. You may deposit with FINCOM a minimum sum of K10,000 or more for periods ranging from one month upwards. Interest rates are attractive. Deposit with FINCOM. Your deposit may also be used as back-up to establish a letter of credit when your cash flow is low. You may also use the interest for other investments whilst the principal amount is earning more. For more information call Business Development Department at 620-477, who will be in a position to receive your money. Bring that extra sum to FINCOM, your first choice in finance.

Conclusion

As can be seen from the analysis above, many Malawian radio commercials, whether advertising commodities like cosmetics or advocating child-spacing, reinforce the idea that a woman cannot and should not make decisions without masculine guidance. Dependence means powerlessness, and 'power is the name of the game' (Westhues 1983, 20). Enabling women to make decisions, for instance, about child-bearing, allows them to allocate time for education, economic and political activities (Haffajee 1995, 11). Other Malawian commercials use women's sexuality as a lure, ignoring their skills and potential in public life.

A final Table (4) is offered below. It shows that a commercial featuring male characters, or both males and females, is more likely to portray females negatively than one portraying females only.

The large number of commercials featuring both female and male voices which denigrate females, shown in Table 4, reflects the widespread and internalised acceptance of gender stereotypes which favour men, in wider Malawian society.

In turn, denigrating women in the media will perpetuate this acceptance; the images of women the media present have a major influence on our ideas of what women are like and how they should behave (Glover 1986). While typical radio commercials are only a few seconds long, and they are said to be unpopular among listeners (discussions with radio staff and listeners 1995), they can cause ripples in listeners' values and perceptions, since the avowed purpose of commercials is that of persuasion. There is no adequate evidence to suggest that MBC, or its advertisers, set out to denigrate women through its radio commercials. ommercials which denigrate women shape and reinforce the women's views of themselves and their place in society. However, by justifying gender inequalities, such commercials persuade society to maintain the women's subordination.

In order to improve the image of women portrayed in radio commercials, at least three things must be done. First, commercials must be designed in such a way that they present images of women, and of gender relations, in a balanced manner. Women must be presented in diverse occupations, and the problems that they may encounter in male-dominated arenas must not be 'conveniently' edited. Second, there is need to increase the female-male ratio among MBC employees who can voice or air commercials. It is clear from the data in Table 4 that one way of improving the images of females in radio commercials in the Malawian context would be to increase the proportion of commercials aired or voiced exclusively by females. Third, training on gender issues in the media, and on non-sexist advertising techniques, could be offered to the staff of radio stations and their advertising clients.

In conclusion, it should be emphasised that radio commercials are obviously not the fundamental cause of the subordinate status of women; nor could this status be changed by the commercials alone. Rather, the causes are deeply rooted in social,

Table 4: Portrayal of females by gender of voice(s) heard

	Gender of voices			
Image of females	Female	Male	Female and male	Total
Negative	0	5	22	27
Positive	6	0	1	7
Negative and positive	3	0	6	9
Neutral	0	48	9	57
Total	9	53	38	100

economic and political structures, as well as in culturally-determined attitudes. However, it is within the power of radio advertising to stimulate change.

Charles D. Chilimampunga is a lecturer in sociology at Chancellor College, a constituent college of the University of Malawi. Contact address: Sociology Department, Chancellor College, PO Box 280, Zomba, Malawi. E-mail: chilimampunga Tel (265) 522-222; fax (265) 522 046.

References

Glover, D (1986) *The Sociology of the Mass Media*, Causeway Press Ltd, Ormskirk.

Goffman, E (1979) *Gender Advertisement*, Macmillan, London.

Haffajee, F (1995) *'Sex education and the school girl'*, Daily Times Newspaper, Blantyre, Malawi, 12 July, p.11.

Henley, NM (1977) *Body Politics: Power, Sex, and Non-verbal Communication*, Prentice-Hall, Englewood Cliffs, NJ.

Hobbs, DA and Blank, SJ (1975) *Sociology and the Human Experience*, John Wiley and Sons Inc, New York.

Kaimila-Kanjo, G (1995) *'The Representation of Women in Malawian Media: a Model for Analysis and Change'*, a paper presented at a UNESCO seminar on Women and the Democratisation Process in Malawi, Blantyre, Malawi, 29-31 May.

Malawi Government (1987) *Malawi Population and Housing Census*, National Statistical Office, Government Print, Zomba.

Posner, J (1987) *'The objectified male: the new male image in advertising'* in Nemiroff, H (ed.) Women and Men: Interdisciplinary Readings on Gender, Fitzhenry and Whiteside, Toronto.

Rappoport, R and Rappoport, RN (1978) *Working Couples*, Routledge and Kegan Paul, London.

Singer, BD (1986) *Advertising and Society*, Addison-Wesley, Don Mills, Ontario.

Tannen, D (1991) *You just don''t understand: Women and men in conversation*, Virago Press, London

Westhues, K (1983) *'Meditation on Newfoundland'*, a paper presented in a Queens College seminar at Memorial University, Canada, February.

UN (1995) *The World's Women: Trends and Statistics*, UN, New York

Zimmerman, DH and West, C (1975) *'Sex roles, interruptions, and silences in conversations'* in Thorne, B and Henley, N (eds.) Language and Sex: Difference and Dominance, Newberry House, Massachussetts.

Resources

Compiled by Emma Pearce

Books and papers

Do it Herself: Women and Technical Innovation, Helen Appleton, IT Publications, 1995.
Women are the majority of small-scale technology users; this title, the outcome of a research project by Intermediate Technology, investigates their contributions to innovation at grassroots level using 22 case studies in Africa, Asia, and Latin America.
IT Publications, 103-105 Southampton Row, London WC1B 4HH, UK. Fax: + 44 (0)171 436 2013.

Gender and indigenous knowledge in various organizations, Helen E Appleton, Catherine LM Hill, provided on the internet at http://www.nuffic.nl/ciran/ ikdm/2-3/ articles/hill.html
This article asserts that a better understanding of local knowledge systems, particularly their gendered nature, can help to make development efforts more effective and sustainable. The article looks at NGOs and international organisations and makes some policy recommendations.

Gender, Small-scale Industry and Development Policy, Isa Baud and GA de Bruijne (eds.), IT Publications, 1993.

Considers the role of small-scale industries in development, in relation to different approaches to the employment of women.

A case study of the footwear industry is analysed by its component activities, using a wide range of technical and practical data.

Women and Food Security: The Experience of the SADCC Countries, Marilyn Carr (ed.), IT Publications, 1991.
A country-by-country study. Women in Southern Africa play a major role in the production, processing, and marketing of food, and are often constrained from fully contributing to the development of this sector by the lack efficient technologies, as well as by lack of access to existing technologies. The experiences described have wide application outside Southern countries.

Whose Development? An ethnography of Aid, Emma Crewe and Elizabeth Harrison, Zed Books, 1998.
Taking technology-based projects as a major focus, this book analyses a number of deep-seated assumptions in the minds of 'developers', describing how power inequalities based on race, class, and gender are reflected in the processes of aid.
Zed Books, 7 Cynthia Street, London N1 9JF, UK. Fax: +44 (0)171 833 3960.

Women @ Internet: Creating New Cultures in Cyberspace, Wendy Harcourt (ed.), Zed Books, 1999.
This fascinating book 'emerges from the cyberculture created by a group of women

and men meeting together in cyberspace' through the Women on the Net project, set up by the Society for International Development with UNESCO funding. Contributions from discuss the scope for using the Internet as a political tool to further the cause of women's equality. The first book to consider these issues from the point of view of women in developing countries, as well as those from industrialised settings.

Gender and Technology: Empowering Women, Engendering Development, Saskia Everts, Zed Books, 1998.
This is an up-to-date introduction to the issue of gender and technology in development. Starting from a commitment to women's rights and gender equity, it discusses practical ways of identifying women's technological needs, and of integrating gender considerations into technology projects. It includes a timely section on the potential for women of working with the private sector.

Women's Roles in the Innovation of Food Cycle Technologies, Ipek Ilkkaracan and Helen Appleton, UNIFEM, 1994.
This source book, published with IT, stresses the importance and scope of women's existing technical experience, highlights the expertise that exists in rural areas, and questions the low status traditionally accorded to women's technical knowledge. The book aims to show development practitioners that in the process of developing technologies, women must be consulted first because they are the real 'experts'.
Women's Ink, 777 United Nations Plaza, New York, NY 10010, USA. Fax: +1 (212) 687 8633; e-mail: wink@womenink.org; website: http://www.womenink.org

Women's Roles in Technical Innovation, Ipek Ilkkarakan and Helen Appleton, UNIFEM, 1995.
Women's indigenous technical knowledge and innovative solutions to problems are in

evidence across the whole range of food cycle technologies. This book gives a brief account of this knowledge and goes on to explore women's role in the innovation process. The arguments are illustrated through case studies and the book includes guidelines for development practitioners working with women.

Trade-Related Employment for Women in Industry and Services in Developing Countries, Susan Joekes, UN Occasional Paper No. 5, 1995.
The paper provides information on the situation in five countries where the project on Technical Co-operation and Women's Lives, run jointly by UNRISD and UNDP, has conducted policy dialogues on issues of gender.
http://www.unrisd.org/engindex/publ/list/opb/opb5/opb5-05.htm

Inventing Women: Science, Technology and Gender, Gill Kirkup and Laurie Smith Keller, Polity Press, in association with the Open University, 1992.
The book aims to introduce students of women's studies to debates in science and technology. The articles are written in an accessible style; topics addressed include third world technology and appropriate technology, and the impact of science and technology on the status of women.
Polity Press, 65 Bridge Street, Cambridge CB2 1UR, UK.

'Innovations in Work Organizations at Enterprise Level, Changes in Technology and Women's Employment', Swasti Mitter, BRIDGE Report 14 1993, IDS.
Analyses the impact of new ways of working and new technologies on women's employment in both the developed and the developing world. The report outlines how different technologies will change patterns in women's employment and concludes that close collaboration of research and policy-making bodies is necessary.

IDS, University of Sussex, Brighton BN1 9RE, UK. Fax: +44 (0)1273 691647. Also at http://kipper.ntd.co.uk/cgi-ids/getbook.dll/138

Missing Links: Gender equity in science and technology for development, Women Encounter Technology: Changing Patterns of Employment in the Third World, Swasti Mitter and Sheila Rowbotham (eds.), Routledge, 1995.
This collection explores the effects of new technologies on women's employment and on the nature of women's work. The editors and contributors are leading scholars in the field of technology and development; the articles document the impact of information technology on the working lives of women in third world countries.
Routledge, 11 New Fetter Lane, London EC4P 4EE, UK. Fax: +44 (0)171 842 2302.

'Re-envisioning Woman, Science and Technology Towards 1995 and Beyond', Programme Proposal, Once and Future Action Network (OFAN), Jan 1995.
Outlines the opportunities that OFAN envisaged for the 1995 UN conference on women and the parallel NGO forum, focusing on the contribution of the World Young Women's Christian Association. (See Organisations section for contact details.)

Technological change and rural development in poor countries: Neglected issues, Kartik C. Roy and Cal Clark (eds.), Oxford University Press, Calcutta, 1994.
Looks at technological change and rural development in India and considers appropriate technology, technology transfer, and women's status in relation to these.
Oxford University Press, Walton Street, Oxford OX2 6DP, UK.
Fax: +44 (0)1865 313925.

Technology, Gender, and Power in Africa, Patricia Stamp, International Development Research Centre (IDRC), Ottawa, 1990.
The author argues that flawed approaches to the links between technology transfer and gender factors, and biases at all levels of policy-making, have led to ineffective or even harmful development projects. Uses case studies from development literature on agriculture, health, and nutrition, as well as from feminist scholarship on Africa and is a technical critique of the sources.
IDRC, 250 Albert Street, PO Box 8500, Ottawa, Ontario, Canada K1G 3H9.

Working Group Report, United Nations Commission on Science and Technology for Development, IDRC, IT Publications and UNIFEM, 1995.
The final report of this working group is presented along with papers from many academics. The aim of the book is to persuade governments, the UN, the scientific community, and NGOs of the need for action and a better understanding of the links between gender, science, technology, and sustainable human development.

Food Cycle Technology Source Books, (1987-93) (series), UNIFEM.
These titles cover small-scale processing of crops in developing countries, in order to provide UNIFEM consultants with technical understanding of traditional and improved technologies for use in these countries. Also offers an illustration of the wider socio-economic context in which such projects are found.
UNIFEM, 304 E 45th Street, 6th floor, New York, NY 10017, USA.
Fax: +1 (212) 906 6705.

EmpowerTools: Technology for Women's Empowerment, UNIFEM, 1995.
This booklet illustrates how technologies can strengthen women's position in their communities. It describes improved cassava processing in Cameroon and Ghana, a Pakistan radio project which provides women with information on available technologies, and related projects in Mozambique and Nigeria. To read the article on the Internet, visit gopher://

gopher.undp.org/00/unifem/public/empo
Many other UNIFEM papers are available
from their website: http://www.wigsat.org

Journals

Appropriate Technology, IT Publications,
London.
This provides development workers with
news, articles, and reports from the field
and carries many gender-related articles.
They have a complete index of articles
concerning women and development
which can be accessed from their website at
http://www.oneworld.org/itdg/journals/
appropriate.html

Gender, Technology and Development, Sage
Publications.
This is an international journal which
explores the linkages between changing
gender relations and technological development. The diverse perspectives of the Asian
region provide the main focus but dialogues
along East-West and North-South lines are
also an important aspect of the journal.
Sage Publications, 6 Bonhill St, London
EC2A 4PU, UK. Fax: +44 (0)171 374 8741

*International Gender, Science and Technology
Digest.*
The *Digest* is a bimonthly newsletter of
activities, meetings, and who's doing what
in gender, science ,and technology,
distributed by e-mail and post. It is also
available on the WIGSAT web site at
http://www.wigsat.org/index.html
To subscribe, send a message to
WIGSAT-L@list.ifias.ca with 'subscribe' in
the subject heading.

Small Enterprise Development, IT Publications.
This journal aims to provide a forum for
those involved in the design and admin-
istration of small enterprise programmes in
less developed countries. It includes new

research, field experience, reviews of relevant material and announcements of forth-
coming conferences and is aimed at
specialists and policymakers in government, banks, and international agencies.

Women and the Information Technology, Issue
No.1/1996 of the UN's Division for the
Advancement of Women (DAW) newsletter
Women2000.
This special issue points out the need for
greater participation by women world-
wide in the use of the new technologies and
argues that if used effectively, these new
technologies have the potential to help
women step out of their isolation and to
support the growing globalisation of the
women's movement. It is available online
at http://www.un.org/womenwatch/
daw/public/w2cont.htm

Organisations

Acacia Initiative
International Development Research
Centre, PO Box 8500, Ottawa, Ontario,
Canada K1G 3H9. Tel: +1 (613) 236 6163
ext. 2605; fax: +1 (613) 567 7749; website:
http://www.idrc.ca/acacia
The Acacia Initiative is part of the International Development Research Centre
(IDRC). Aims to enable sub-Saharan African
communities to apply information and
communication technologies to their social
and economic development. Acacia will
work mainly with rural and disadvantaged
communities, and particularly their women
and youth groups.

Acceso Foundation
Fundaciûn Acceso, San José, Costa Rica.
Tel: +506 224 6076; fax: +506 283 2748;
website: http://www.acceso.org/
This is a private, not-for-profit technical
assistance organisation dedicated to
increasing opportunities for the poor and

disenfranchised in Central America to participate meaningfully in decisions and institutions that affect their lives. Acceso is especially active in the fields of sustainable development, human rights/civil liberties, women's programmes, and employment and income generation. The website is in English and Spanish.

African Resource Centre for Indigenous Knowledge (ARCIK)
Nigerian Institute of Social and Economic Research, PMB 5, U.I. Post Office, Ibadan, Nigeria. Tel: +234 (22) 440 0501-5; fax: +234 (22) 400 550-79
ARCIK is a resource centre which documents and disseminates information on indigenous knowledge in Africa. The centre is interested in exploring gender in relation to indigenous knowledge and decision-making, indigenous organisations, and indigenous approaches to creativity, innovation and experimentation reflecting local responses to priority problems.

Appropriate Technology and Project Management in Developing Countries (ATOL)
Blijde Inkomststraat 9, 3000 Leuven, Belgium. Tel: +32 (16) 224 517, fax: +32 (16) 222 256; website: http://www.atol. ngonet.be/engels/eatol.htm
ATOL is an independent and non-profit service centre created in 1976. It provides assistance to individuals and organisations which are involved in development co-operation and North/South relations. Its services include provision of information, research, training and consultancy and it is active in the area of gender.

Do-It-Herself (DIH): Women and Technological Innovation Programme
Attention Helen Appleton, Myson House, Railway Terrace, Rugby CV 21 3HT, UK.
Tel: +44 (788) 560 631; fax: +44 (788) 540 270
DIH is a global research and advocacy programme co-ordinated by the ITDG's

Bangladesh, Peru, Sri Lanka, Sudan, UK, and Zimbabwe offices in collaboration with UNIFEM. Recognising that women's local technical knowledge and skills have been undervalued, the programme promotes strategies to ensure equal access for women and men to resources, services, and training.

Gender, Science and Development Programme (GSD)
39 Spadina Road Toronto, Ontario, Canada M5R 2S9. Website: http://www.ifias.ca/ GSD/GSDinfo.html
This is one of the collaborative policy research and advocacy programmes of the International Federation of Institutes for Advanced Study. The programme studies and makes policy recommendations on the effects of science and technology on the lives of women. It emphasises North-South co-operation in understanding the role women play in the development and application of science and technology, and studies ways of increasing women's contribution to science and development.

Gender and Science and Technology Association, (GASAT)
Website: http://www.wigsat.org/gasat/ gasat8.html (currently under construction)
GASAT is an international association concerned with the interactions between gender and science and technology. The theme of its eighth international conference (held in Ahmedabad, India, in January 1996) was: 'Towards Sustainable Development? Achieving Four Es: Education, Employment, Equality, Empowerment.' The papers presented can be viewed or downloaded from their website.

Ghana Regional Appropriate Technology Industrial Service (GRATIS)
PO Box 151, Tema, Ghana.
Tel: +233 (221) 4243
GRATIS, a regional NGO involved in the development and dissemination of small-scale and intermediate technologies for

grassroots producers, provides urban and rural women with technical support in their productive activities, using participatory methodologies.

Instituto de Estudios Regionales Ayacucho (IERA)
Urb. Maria Parado do Bellido G1-16, Casilla do Correos No 60, Ayacucho, Peru.
IERA focuses on research, documentation, advocacy, dissemination, training, and networking activities in the area of traditional agriculture and technology, traditional medicine, health, nutrition, and the environment, with specific attention to women's knowledge, and their productive and reproductive roles.

Intermediate Technology Development Group (ITDG),
Myson House, Railway Terrace, Rugby CV 21 3HT, UK. Tel: +44 (788) 560 631; fax: +44 (788) 540 270; website: www.oneworld.org/itdg/index.html
ITDG is an international development agency which works with rural communities in Africa, Asia, and Latin America. It aims to enable poor people in the South to develop and use skills and technologies which give them more control over their lives and which contribute to sustainable development. It regards development as a process of increasing people's economic power by improving their access to technologies appropriate to their skills, incomes, and environments. ITDG has offices in Bangladesh, Kenya, Nepal, Peru, Sri Lanka, Sudan, and Zimbabwe.

International Women's Tribune Centre (IWTC)
77 UN Plaza, New York, NY 10017, USA. Tel: +1 (212) 687 8633; fax: +1 (212) 661 2704; website: http://www.igc.org/beijing/ngo/iwtc.html
IWTC is an information and communication support group for women's and community organisations in Africa, Asia, Latin America, Western Asia, the Caribbean, and the South Pacific. Its quarterly newsletter, *The Tribune*, and other action-oriented publications offer strategies for action and resources in four main areas: information and communication, science and technology, women organising, and community economic development. Science and technology is a major programme, with emphasis on demystifying and popularising science and technology.

Kenya Engergy and Environment Organisation (KENGO)
Natural Resources Research and Development Programme, PO Box 48197, Nairobi, Kenya.
Tel: +254 (2) 748 281; fax: +254 (2) 749 382
KENGO is a coalition of grassroots women's groups involved in research and community development activities using appropriate technologies and locally available resources.

Once and Future Action Network, (OFAN)
Secretariat, Business District, 40, Duke St, Kingston, Jamaica.
Tel: +1 (809) 967 2399 fax: +1 (809) 967 2397; website: http://www.wigsat.org/ofan/ofan.html
This is a growing NGO network which seeks to reclaim women's traditional and rich knowledge of resource management, environmental conservation, and 'science for survival', and to promote women's contribution to redirecting science and technology for a sustainable future. The concerns of the many organisations involved range from reforming curricula, to interest girls in science and technology, to networking among women scientists.

Programme for Appropriate Technology in Health (PATH)
PATH, 4 Nickerson Street, Seattle, WA 98109-1699, USA.
Tel: +1 (206) 285 3500; fax: +1 (206) 285 6619; website: http://www.path.org

Among PATH's goals are improving the availability and use of appropriate diagnostic technologies, of appropriate protective/ preventive technologies, improving women's health, and addressing the special needs of girls. Their website has many case studies.

Servicios Multiples de Technologias Apropiadas (SEMTA)
Casilla 15401, La Paz, Bolivia.
Tel: +591 (2) 360042; fax: +591(2) 391458
This national NGO is involved in technology development and dissemination with rural women, using participatory methodologies with specific attention to women's indigenous technologies, and local agricultural and ecological systems. South-South technology transfer, women's ownership of technology development initiatives, and support of women's own innovations, constitute the main focus of SEMTA's work.

Swiss Centre for Appropriate Technology (SKAT)
Vadianstrasse 42 CH-9000 St. Gallen Switzerland. Tel: +41 71 228 54 54, fax: +41 71 228 54 55, web site http://www.skat.ch/
SKAT is a leading Swiss consultancy firm and documentation centre working internationally in the areas of water and sanitation, architecture and building, transport infrastructure, and urban development. Since 1978, SKAT has collected relevant information on appropriate technologies, documented lessons learned, and disseminated them in partnership with institutions and individuals in developing countries.

TOOL
TOOL Foundation, Sarphatistraat 650, 1018 AV Amsterdam, The Netherlands.
Tel: +31 20 626 44 09, fax: 31 20 627 74 89; web site: http://www.tool.nl/
Tool's main objective is to facilitate information exchange between organisations and individuals in developing countries who want to share their knowledge and experience. Emphasis is on practical, small-scale, innovative technology projects in developing countries, small-scale enterprises, innovation processes, environmentally sound technologies and the position of women. Tool is will soon be transferring its activities to other organisations. TOOL's question-and-answer service will move to Agromisa, also in Wageningen. The major part of TOOL's documentation centre will move to the Uganda Rural Development and Training Programme (URDT).

The Third World Organization for Women in Science (TWOWS)
Enrico Fermi Building, Room 109, Via Beirut 6, 34014 Trieste, Italy. Web site: http://www.ictp.trieste.it/~twas/TWOWS.html
TWOWS is an independent, not-for-profit NGO based at the offices of the Third World Academy of Sciences (TWAS) in Trieste, Italy. TWOWS is the first international forum to unite eminent women scientists from the South with the objective of strengthening their role in the development process and promoting their representation in scientific and technological leadership.

Gender Advisory Board, UN Commission on Science and Technology for Development (UNCSTD)
http://www.wigsat.org/gab/uncstd.htm
The Gender Advisory Board was established by UNCSTD to ensure that gender issues are adequately addressed in all its future deliberations. The topic 'Gender, Science, Technology and Sustainable Human Development' was selected by UNCSTD in 1993 as one of three topics relating to the science and technology components of major UN Conferences held in 1995. The Fourth World Conference on Women and Development, held in Beijing in 1995, was one such major conference. A

Gender Working Group was therefore formed to analyse the implications of science and technology, sustainable human development, and gender.

United Nations Research Institute for Social Development (UNRISD)
Gentech, Palais des Nations, 1211 Geneva 10 Switzerland; website: http://www.unrisd. org/engindex/research/rescurr3.htm# (UNRISD) is an autonomous agency engaging in multi-disciplinary research on the social dimensions of contemporary problems affecting development. The Institute attempts to provide governments, development agencies, grassroots organisations and scholars with a better understanding of how development policies and processes of economic, social and environmental change affect different social groups. One of its current research programmes is 'Technical Co-operation and Women's Lives: Integrating Gender into Development Policy'. The overarching objective of the project has been to enhance the gender sensitivity of development policies, with a particular focus on macro-economic policies.

Internet resources

Africa Online
http://www.africaonline.com
Africa Online provides internet communications services throughout Africa. Information can be searched for, country by country or under the site's various service areas. The women's area has links to a large number of African and international women's organisations.

BRIDGE (Briefings on development and gender)
http://www.ids.ac.uk/bridge/index.html
BRIDGE is an innovative information and analysis service specialising in gender and

development issues. BRIDGE's objective is to assist development professionals and organisations to integrate gender concerns into their work.

The British Library for Development Studies at IDS, University of Sussex
http://www.ids.ac.uk/blds/index.html
Europe's largest and most comprehensive research collection on development. Its extensive collection of government publications, journals, and the published outputs of NGOs and research institutes worldwide is supplemented by substantial holdings of UN and WTO publications (for which BLDS has deposit library status).

Eldis
http://nt1.ids.ac.uk/eldis/gender/gen_lele.htm
Eldis is a means of accessing on-line information on development and the environment. Eldis focuses on countries of the South and structures the selection of materials for easy access. It is hosted by the Institute of Development Studies, Sussex (see above for the website address of its gender section).

The Gender Advisory Board of the UN Commission on Science and Technology for Development (UNCSTD)
http://www.wigsat.org/gab/uncstd.htm
The Gender Advisory Board was established by UNCSTD to ensure that gender issues are adequately addressed in all its future deliberations, and as part of its mandate the Gender Working Group (GWG) was asked to review the performance of UN agencies in the domain of gender, science, and technology. This site contains its recommendations and links to other organisations and policy documents.

Gender and Technology Resources
http://www.postindustrial.com/morewomen/resources.html
This is a useful website supplied by the Independent Committee on Women and

Global Knowledge, an alliance of nine network organisations based in Ontario, Canada. The site has many links to relevant and up-to-date papers and organisations.

Gender Net
http://www.worldbank.org/gender/
This site describes how the World Bank group promotes gender equality. It has links to many other World Bank sites and provides useful information on its programmes and projects. Its search function takes the user to a large amount of information on technology in these projects.

Gender, Science and Technology: An International Bibliography
http://www.wigsat.org/bib.html
This is an excellent resource listing approximately 70 relevant titles from a wide range of authors.

Information Services @ ids
http://nt1.ids.ac.uk/
This is a site hosted by the Institute of Development Studies, Sussex which is an invaluable resource for researching many issues relating to gender and development - it includes links to Eldis, The British Library for Development Studies at IDS, and Bridge (see above).

International Gender, Science and Technology Map
http://www.wigsat.org/gstpmap.html
A well organised index of institutions, resources, and research material.

The Institute for Women and Technology
http://www.parc.xerox.com/oct/projects/iwt.org/otherorgs.html
This website lists, describes, and provides links to, many organisations around the world that are working to improve the situation for women who are active in technology-related disciplines, and to increase the number and impact of women working in those fields.

Miningco.com
http://women3rdworld.miningco.com/
This regularly updated site aims to provide quickly the best links to selected subject areas. It has a wealth of information on women's issues and has a special area and search function for women's issues in the third world.

Open University Gender & Technology Study Group:
http://mcs.open.ac.uk/gentech/gtothersites.html
This provides many links to sites and papers concerning women and technology and also has some development links, for instance to a site called 'Women and Minorities in Science and Engineering' at http://www.ai.mit.edu/people/ellens/Gender/wom_and_min.html

The Pier
http://www.sussex.ac.uk/Units/library/pier/subjects.dir/socs.dir/gender.html#science
This is an Internet archive set up by the University of Sussex. It has a great many resources and an area dedicated to women and science and technology.

UNRISD-On Line
http://www.unrisd.org/
As part of its function of promoting original research, the United Nations Research Institute for Social Development (UNRISD) has set up this on-line service. It provides links to a large number of papers and publications on gender issues and to information about the UNRISD/UNDP project on Technical Co-operation and Women's Lives.

WIGSAT-L
http://www.wigsat.org/it.html
This is an Internet mailing list on international gender, science and technology issues, for NGOs, researchers, policy makers and anyone interested in

gender, science, and technology for development. The list regularly distributes information on job announcements, events, and publications.

WIGSAT Women in Global Science and Technology
http://www.wigsat.org
This site acts as an electronic information bridge between the major global gender, science, and technology initiatives. WIGSTAT aims to facilitate global networking among women scientists and technologists on critical issues in science and technology for development and to promote policy advocacy and action which recognizes and supports women's contributions to science and technology for development.

Women and Development Online Information Project
http://www.sfc.keio.ac.jp/~thiesmey/wid english.html
This is an academic information database and search engine which uses data from Thailand, Vietnam, China, and Japan on modernisation and gender in Asia and the Asian diaspora. The information is available free of charge and the aim is to make the database as comprehensive and easy to use as possible. There are project reports and information about participating organisations and several bibliographies currently under construction.

Women Watch, 'The Internet Gateway on the Advancement and Empowerment of Women'
http://www.un.org/womenwatch/
This is a joint initiative of the UN's International Research and Training Institute for the Advancement of Women (INSTRAW), the Division for the Advancement of Women (DAW), the Development Fund For Women (UNIFEM) the Sustainable Development Networking Programme (SDNP), the Gender in Development Programme and the World Bank and the Spanish Instituto de la Mujer. It is a convenient way of searching the websites of all the organisations involved from one starting point.

Electronic discussion groups

Electronic discussion conference WomenSciTech.
An open conference for the discussion of any topic related to gender, science, and technology. To subscribe, send an e-mail to WST-L@list.ifias.ca with 'subscribe' in the subject heading.